THE METHOD AND THE PSYCHOANALYSIS THEORY

BY
CLAUDIO GARCIA CAPITAO

© MMVIII. All Rights Reserved.

This book is printed on acid-free paper.

Copyright © 2008 Claudio Garcia Capitao. All rights reserved.

Published by Aberdeen University Press Services.

No part of this book shall be reproduced, stored in a retrieval system, or transmitted by any means, electronic, mechanical, photocopying, recording, or otherwise, without written permission from the publisher. No patent liability is assumed with respect to the use of the information contained herein. Although every precaution has been taken in the preparation of this book, the publisher assumes no responsibility for errors or omissions.

Every effort has been made to make this book as complete and as accurate as possible, but no warranty or fitness is implied. This information provided is on an "as is" basis. The publisher shall have neither liability nor responsibility to any person or entity with respect to any misguidance or misunderstanding from the information contained in the book.

Printed in the United States of America

ISBN: 978-0-6152-1556-3

This book is printed on 8" x 11", perfect binding, 60# cream interior paper, black and white interior ink, 100# white exterior paper, full-color exterior ink. Prices are subject to change.

Cover Title Designed by Aberdeen University Press Services.

THE METHOD AND THE PSYCHOANALYSIS THEORY
First Edition

Claudio Garcia Capitao

DEDICATION

This book is dedicated to professors,
my patients and my students.

ABSTRACT

The present work had as a goal to show how the method Psychoanalytic has a fundamental importance for the Psychoanalysis Theory and Technique. From a theoretical study about the psychoanalytical theory especially the main ideas of Sigmund Freud to boarding a modern theory about the method, in other words, the Fields Theory. Freud and the psychoanalytical school discovered a dimension of the human psychology that revolutionized our knowledge on the being psychic dynamic nature, putting the discovered the imaginary and the fantasies world that represent the drive. After the basic ideas have been boarded, it sought to clarify the main methodological operation of the psychoanalysis occurs the interpretation. It searched through of the understanding Field and of Rupture of Field, explain some clinical implications like the transit expectation and the effect vortex, as well as the representation concepts. They presented the psychotherapy techniques and their goals, as well as examples of clinical cases extracted of the literature and of the assistance in psychotherapy.

TABLE OF CONTENTS

1. Introduction 01
   1.1. *The Psychoanalytical Theory* 01
   1.2. *First And Second Topics In Short* 01
2. The Psychoanalysis Method 19
   2.1. *Psychoanalytical Field: An Approach* 19
   2.2. *Field and Field's Rupture* 23
   2.3. *The Rupture In The "Fesh"* 26
   2.4. *Unconscious: Some Consideration* 28
   2.5. *A Brief Incursion In Another Field* 34
3. The Interpretation In The Psychoanalysis: The Method Essence 37
4. Theoretical Application 44
   4.1. *A Brief Evaluation Of The Sexual Violence: Oedipus Revenge* 44
   4.2. *A First Approach: The Symptom Of The Social* 45
   4.3. *Search Soul Of The Violence* 46
   4.4. *The Psychoanalysis And The Soul Demons* 48
5. From The Depression To The Suicide 55
   5.1. *The Several Depression Understanding Searches* 56
   5.2. *Depression In Childhood* 64
   5.3. *Depression In The Adolescence* 66
   5.4. *A Modern Theory: Fields' Theory* 73
   5.5. *Interpretation And Representation: Field And Rupture* 76
6. The Psychological Clinic And Their Cases 79
   6.1. *Clinical Cases* 79
       Clinical Case I: Maria's Case 88
       Clinical Case II: The Scratch 96
       Clinical Case III: CID 10 98
       Clinical Case IV: The Big Proof 100
       Clinical Case V: Organic Implication 102
       Clinical Case VI: The Rape 105
7. Final Considerations 111
Appendex – I: Bibliographic References 113
Appendex – II: About Author 117
Appendex – III: Index 119

Chapter 1
Introduction

1. Introduction

1.1. The Psychoanalytical Theory

1.2. First and Second Topics in Short

The psychology history does not fail to demonstrate that since Freud the center of gravity of all psychology dislocated. The object of study psychoanalysis became the person psychic life depth, in other words, it's unconscious. Without any surplus for the doubt meet, in the psychology Freudian, empiricism and associationism traces (the action structuration theory of the external circumstances of the infantile life), that allowed an approach between psychoanalytical theory and for reflexology and behaviorism, however, the essential of the psychological conception of Freud built a dynamic psychology or psychodynamic of the forces that compose the unconscious of the person. The unconscious acquires there a place of such a highlight that tends not only to subject the conscious, as well as to subdue it (Ey, 1977).

The psychoanalysis it came back deliberately for impulses and the archaic forms of primitive existence whose "thirst" is the unconscious, has not interest by the "forms" and functions "of the psychic life (language, thought, behavior like schools behaviorist) safe in the that these express and symbolize the unconscious forces of which are, so to speak, simply effect. Thus, it has in the dream the prototype of the symbolic imaginary production of the unconscious that constitutes the investigations field of the analytic psychology. In this production, the images submitted to the laws of the unconscious thought (emphasize symbolic, condensation, displacement, content substitution manifest relatively to the latent content), Freud and the psychoanalytical school discovered a dimension of the human psychology that revolutionized our knowledge on being's psychic dynamic nature, putting to discovered the imaginary and the ghosts world that represent impulses. Another fundamental aspect is the psychoanalysis fact consider person's past not just like the memory content", but like a still alive layer of experiences that, even unconscious, and above all, this way, intervene in the situations ideas and current feeling. Thence the development phases importance of the psychic life and above all of the succession of the instinctive-affective phases pre-genital, after genital (or oedipal) that, more or less repressed, come in the individual personality constitution (Ey, 1977).

In 1909 for Clark University, in Worcester, Massachusetts, commemorated its twentieth year of its foundation, and your president, the Dr. G. Stanley Hall, invited Freud and some of your main followers to take part in the commemoration and to receive honorary titles. The five Freud's Conferences had beginning on Monday, 6 of

September of 1909e, and they prosecuted in the four subsequent days. The conferences, following a Freud's Old Habit, were pronounced on the spur of the moment and almost without previous preparation. Only after your return to Vienna him was armature to writes them, in dislike. During its entire career Freud was always ready to expose his discoveries. Despite increases that should be done to the psychoanalysis structure in the twenty-five years that were followed, these conferences give an admirable square preliminary that demands much little correction. Still give an easiness and clearness excellent idea and of the easy-going sense so that they did of Freud a notable lecturer (editor note, 1957).

Without using of the hypnosis Freud managed to obtain from the patients that that I was necessary to establish the relation among pathogenic scenes forgotten and the symptoms that emerged quickly associates to the material not yet forgotten. There was some force that prevented that they became conscious and compelled to what they remained unconscious. The force that I kept the pathological state stayed under the resistance form by the patient. It was about this resistance idea that Freud based his points of view on events' psychic course in the hysteria. The patients' hysterical investigation and of other neurotic led him to the conclusion that repression of the idea to which links the intolerable wish failed. It is very true that they managed to leave the conscience and of the memory and apparently liberated of a displeasure enormous quantity. But the loaded impulse of wish that it was emphasized it continues to there be in the unconscious (Freud, 1910/1996)

In the patient in treatment, two forces enter operation, one against to another: Of your side conscious effort to bring to the conscience the idea forgotten in the unconscious of the emphasized material and of its derivatives. For Freud (1910/1996). The psychoanalytical researches that does raise consistently the disease symptoms the impressions of the erotic life, show that the pathogenic impulses loaded of wish they belong to the components compulsive of nature erotic. They will be the childhood experiences that would explain for susceptibility the future traumas and is only by the discovery of these memory traces forgotten, becoming conscious, that we acquire the power of liberate us of the symptoms. These strong impulses loaded of wish they are described how sexual. The main source of infantile sexual pleasure is the excitation adequate of some parts of the especially susceptible body to the stimulation, besides genital organs also has the orifices urethral, anal and oral, as well as the skin and other sensitive surfaces. The satisfaction, it call auto-eroticism, it is obtained in the individual's own body. Suck the finger (sensual suction) is a satisfaction auto-erotic good example of a zone erotic. Direct inhibitions in the development of the sexual function include the perversions and infantilism general in the sexual life. The impulse that remains independent leads to a perversion and can do of its own sexual goal a substitute of the normal goal. The predisposition for the neurosis also can be repaired to the prejudiced sexual development.

Thus for Freud (1909/1996), the human beings get sick when the satisfaction of its erotic needs is frustrated by the reality, wants be for external obstacles or for internal fault of adaptation. They seek refuge in the disease, of way to can find a satisfaction to take the place of that that was frustrated. The pathological symptoms constitute this way, an individual sexual activity bit or even the totality of its sexual life, the reality dismissal is the disease main goal, but it also is the main damage for her caused. The resistance to the cure composes of several reasons. The escape of the unsatisfactory reality for the disease follows the way to involution, of the regression, of a return to a more primitive phase of the sexual life. In every psychoanalytical treatment of a neurotic patient arises the strange called phenomenon transfer. The patient drives to the doctor a certain degree of affectionate feeling that not if deep on the real relation between both and that only can be originating of old fantasies that were become unconscious. The unconscious wishes liberated by the psychoanalysis can follow several ways. First, the wishes can be broken by the rational mental activity of the pulses how better are opposed to him. Other possibility is that the revealed unconscious pulses can become employed in useful purposes that would have been found earlier if did not have there been an interruption in the development. A third possibility is individual's personal happiness.

In *Besides the Pleasure principle,* (Freud, 1920/1996) takes over that the mental events are regulated automatically by the pleasure principle. The course of these events is invariably unchained by an unpleasant tension. The final result coincides with a decrease of this tension. The mental device it makes an effort to keep the quantity of present excitations in a level as low as possible. Under s auto preservation pulses influence the ego, the pleasure principle goes being substituted by the reality principle. Another mould even the displeasure liberation meets in the conflicts and dissensions that occur in the mental device while the ego is passing by its development for more complex organizations. Most pleasure that we try is perceptive displeasure. The dreams study can be considered as the safest method in investigation of the profound mental processes. The dreams that occur in the traumatic neurosises have the characteristic of making the patient returns repeatedly to the situation of his accident, a situation of which he awakes of terror and fright. A child 1 year and half invented a game that was related with child's great cultural accomplishment; The renouncement to impulse satisfaction, that did when allowing your mother removed herself without anything protest. At the beginning, the child was in a passive situation; but, repeating the joke, although it was unpleasant, passed for an active role. It is not necessary to presuppose the existence of a impulse special imitative so as to supply a reason for the joke. It concludes how same under the pleasure principle domain, exists always manners and enough means to turn what it is unpleasant in a theme the recalled being and elaborated by the mind.

The psychoanalysis above all is an interpretation art. It another goal arises: Make the patient confirms the construction of his memory made by the analyst. The main emphasis is in the patient's resistances: The art consists in discovered them as soon as possible, indicate them to the patient and induced him to abandon such resistances.

However the patient cannot if remind of all that is emphasized itself, what he does not manage to remind can be precisely the essential part. The patient stays obligated to repeat the material emphasized instead of it recalls him like something belonging to past. These reproductions always refer to some portion of the sexual life. When the things arrive to this apprenticeship, can-if tell that the previous neurosis was substituted by the transfer neurosis. The psychoanalyst should get that the patient re-experiencing some parts of your life forgotten but should provide so that the patient maintains certain distance degree. The resistance of the conscious and unconscious ego operates under pleasure principle influence: Search avoid the displeasure that could be produced by the liberation of the emphasized. The initial bloom of the infantile sexual life is predestined to the extinction because your wishes are incompatible with the reality and with the inadequate apprenticeship of development that the child reached. The patients repeat all the unwished situations and painful emotions in the transfer and revive them with the biggest ingenuousness. What the psychoanalysis also reveals in the transfer phenomena of the neurotic can be observed in the lives of some normal people: Those whose human relations have the same effect (Freud, 1920/1996).

The psychoanalytical formulation take it as starting point the impression that the conscience cannot be the universal attribute of the mental processes, but just special function of them. The conscience product consists essentially of excitations perceptions that result from of the outer world and of pleasure and displeasure sensations that arise inside the mental device. The conscious system it characterizes by the peculiarity that in it the processes excitatory do not let any permanent change in their elements but they finish in the phenomenon of become conscious. The alive nucleus is provided of a shield against the stimulus of the outer world. The near cortical layer to the shield should be differentiated like an organ to receive the external stimulus. These cortices sensitive, that afterwards becomes the conscious system, also receives arising excitations of the exterior. The displeasure of the physical pain probably is the result of breaking of the protective shield. There is then a continuous flow of excitations by the relative periphery to the mind's central device, just as could usually arise only of the device interior. The investment energy is summoned of all the even sides to provide an enough investment rose of energy in the rupture surroundings. It establishes one against-investment in great scale and the other psychic systems weaken, so that the psychic functions stay paralyzed or widely reduced. The common traumatic neurosis is considered a consequence of a widespread rupture in the protective shield against the stimulus. The anguish promptness state and super-investment of the receptive systems constitute defense's shield last line against the stimulus. The dreams, of a certain mould, they make an effort to for dominate the stimulus retrospectively; developing the anguish whose omission was the cause of the traumatic neurosis. An exception to the proposal that the dreams are the wishes satisfaction consists in the dreams that occur in the traumatic neurosises; they arise in obedience to the compulsion to the repetition. This way, it would seem that the dreams function, that consists in put aside any reasons that can interrupt the sleep, satisfying the pulses disturbers wishes, is not its original function.

There is something besides the pleasure principle, and then also there was a time before the dreams goal is the wishes accomplishment (Freud, 1910/1996).

The impulses that come of drive do not belong to type of linked nervous processes but they are freely furniture that pressure to find discharge. The manifestations of a compulsion to repeat there are in high degree a character impulse and, when they act in opposition to the pleasure principle, give the aspect of some demonic force in action. It seems that for drive is an inherent need, in the organic life, to restore a previous state of things that the alive entity was obligated to abandon under pressure of external forces disturbers. Drive that direct the destinies of the elementary organisms that survive to the individual as one all, that gives you a safe shelter when they are defenseless against the world exterior, that stimulus make are with other cells germinatives, etc., constitute drive group sexual. These drives are specifically conservative in its resistance to the external influences and preserve life itself. Apart drives sexual not other that do not try to restore a previous state of things. Both a high development and an involution can be consequences of adaptation to the pressure of external forces; in both cases, the role performed by drives can limit itself to the retention of a modification compulsory. What appears on the individuals' majority like an indefatigable pulse for the perfection can be comprehended as a result of repression of impulses on which bases all that it is more precious in the human civilization? For impulses emphasized never ceases to fighting for a complete satisfaction (Freud, 1910/1996).

In fact, impulses of the ego exercise a pressure in the death meaning while impulses sexual exercise pressure in life prolongation meaning. There is the hypothesis that impulses of the ego arise of the fact of the inanimate matter to become lively, and they seek to restore the state of previous inanimate while impulses sexual aim at the gamete conjugation. Without this union the cell dies. Thence the supposition that the death is internal (natural). The psychoanalysis observed the regularity with which the libido removes of the object and drives to the ego. Studying children's development libidinal, it arrived to the conclusion that the ego is the true reservoir and libido original, and that only is from this reservoir that on the libido extends to the objects. That a part of impulses of the ego was seen is libidinal and that impulses sexual act in the ego. This way, the distinction between both impulses changed of qualitative for topographical. It cannot attribute to the impulse sexual the characteristic of a compulsion to repeat. The dominant tendency of the mental life is the effort to reduce, keep constant, or to remove the internal tension owed to the stimulus, a tendency that finds expression at the beginning of the pleasure. The recognition of this fact, for Freud, is important reason for think of death drive existence. One of the first and more important functions of the mental device is to contain the pulses that impinge you, substitute the secondary process and to convert its energy of free investment and in action in a predominantly linked investment. The pleasure principle is a tendency that operates for service of a function to liberate the mental device of excitation or to keep the quantity of constant excitation as lower as possible (Freud, 1910/1996).

Freud's Formulations described above suffered several modifications. However, these formulations were the center for countless theoretical unfolding and of strategies psychotherapeutic conduction and of the researches development. Mostly, it would like to observe with more vehemence, at school Klein.

(In The Ego and the ID, Freud, 1923/1996) reaffirms that the psyche division in conscious and unconscious is the fundamental premise of the psychoanalysis; Only this turns possible to the psychoanalysis understand the pathological processes in the mental life, that are so common as important, and to find a place for them in the science structure. Be conscious is, first, a term purely descriptive, based on perception of the more immediate and defined character. A psychic element is not, usually, conscious for a period of prolonged times. There are mental processes or very powerful ideas that can produce all the effects in the mental life that the original ideas produce, although do not become conscious. The reason which these ideas cannot become conscious is that a certain force is opposed to them; could otherwise become conscious, and it would be then looks to little difference that have regarding other admittedly psychic elements. The state in which the ideas existed before being conscious is called repression, and can affirm that the force that instituted such repression and keeps it is realized like a resistance during the analysis. We obtain the concept of unconscious from repression theory. It is called pre-conscious the latent that is unconscious only in terms of descriptive and does not have dynamic meaning. It restricts the unconscious term to the unconscious dynamically emphasized. In each person there is a coherent organization of the mental processes call ego. The conscience is linked to this ego. The ego controls the accesses to the action and of this ego process to repression by means of which try to exclude some mind's tendencies not only of the conscious but of other affectivity and activity moulds. The resistance, that also s finds in the ego, is unconscious, and floodgate itself like the emphasized. A part of the ego can be unconscious, and this ego unconsciousness is not latent like it pre-conscious (Freud, 1923/1996).

All knowledge that we own is invariably linked to the conscience. We can arrive even to know the unconscious (Ics) by the simple fact of turning it conscious. The conscience is the surface of the mental device. All the perceptions that are received of outside and of inside are conscious (Cs). The real difference between an unconscious idea and an idea pre-conscious (PCs) consists in that the first if prosecutes about material that remains unconscious, while the last (PCs), put in connection with the representations, they are memories residues. They were previously perceptions and as all the mnemonic residues can become again conscious. It thinks of memory residues as being contained in directly adjacent systems to the conscious perceptive system (Pcpt-Cs), so that the investment of these residues can quickly extend until the last system elements. The distinction between Cs and PCs does not have meaning in that concern to the feeling. PCs disappear and the feeling is Cs or Ics. It can consider the individual like an ID psychic, unknown and unconscious, in whose surface the ego reposes, developing, starting from its nucleus, the perceptive system. Illustratively, the ego does not involve the ID, just does it in the measure in which the perceptive system its form surface. The ego not sharply separated of the ID however partially it melts. The emphasized ego also dilutes in the ID, and it just is a part. The ego is the part of the ID that was modified by the direct influence of the outer world through the perceptive-conscious system. In certain meaning is a surface differentiation extension. The ego is before and above all a corporeal ego. Not only what is inferior as well as what is elevated most in ego can be unconscious (Freud, 1923/1996).

Also the ego or superego ideal is not strongly linked to the conscious. The transformation of a choice of erotic object in an ego alteration is a method by the the ego can obtain control on the ID. The object libido' transformation in libido narcissistic implies in an abandonment of the sexual objects. Behind the ego ideal hides the most important identification in the individual, its identification with the father in the own personal history. In both sexes, the relative form of the masculine sexual and feminine disposition sets whether the result of Oedipus complex will be identification with the father or with the mother. The wider general result of the phase dominated by Oedipus complex is the formation of one precipitated in the ego, consisting of two identifications: Of the identification with the father and of the identification with the mother, united to each other somehow. The ego modification maintains its special position; it confronts the other ego contents like an ego or superego ideal. Superego is not an object first choices simple residue of the ID. It represents a reaction energetic formation against these choices. The ego ideal is Oedipus complex heir. It is easy to demonstrate that the ego ideal answers the all that if natures wait elevated most of the man.

For Freud (1923/1996), two impulses classes are differentiated. Impulses sexual or Eros, who is from far in excess evident and accessible to the study, and comprehends not only free impulses sexual properly told and the pulses for inhibited goals or of sublimated nature that of her derive, as well as of the auto preservation instinct. The second impulses class is denominated of impulse of death. It seems that, as a result of the unicellular combination of organisms in life multi cellular forms, for impulse of death of the individual cell can be neutralized with success and impulses destructive can be diverted for the outer world through a special organ. The sadistic component of impulse sexual would be a classical example of a coalition of impulses useful and the sadism that was become independent as a perversion would be typical of a separation. Love generally comes accompanied by the hatred (ambivalence). In the human relations, the hatred is frequently a love precursor. It seems plausible to suppose that the energy dislocated and neutral, that undoubtedly is active in the ego and in the ID, proceed of the reserve narcissi of libido that is Eros desexualized. This libido dislocated is employed for pleasure principle service to avoiding blockades and to facilitate discharges. The energy dislocated also can be defined like sublimated energy. The ego erotic libido transformation involves an abandonment of the sexual objects, a desexualization.

In the set of your new formulations on the mental device, Freud (1923/1996) says that the Ego constitutes of identifications that take the investments place abandoned by the ID. The first these identifications, superego, owes its special position regarding the ego to two factors: It was the first identification and occurred while the ego still was fragile and to for being Oedipus complex heir. Superego is always close to the ID and can act like its representative close to the ego. Part of the feeling of blame usually remains unconscious, because the conscience origin is intimately linked to Oedipus complex that is part to the unconscious. A feeling of blame expresses of different mould under different terms. The feeling of conscious normal blame, it bases on tension between ego and the ego ideal. The feeling of blame is extremely conscious in the obsessive neurosises and in the melancholy but it remains unconscious in the hysteria. The obsessive neurotic, in contrast to the melancholic, never accomplishes a self-destruction act. The ID is totally amoral and the ego fight to be moral and superego can be super moral and then if you become so cruel as only the ID can be. The ego renders services and is threatened by three dangers: By the outer world, by the libido of the ID, and by the superego severity. The great importance that the feeling of blame has in the neurosises turns conceivable that the common neurotic anguish be reinforced in the serious cases by appearance of the anguish between ego and superego. The ID does not have ways to show the ego be love or hatred.

Freud's Most interesting these New Formulations is his affirmation of there is unconscious feeling. It seems, in fact a contradiction, because the feeling is in the order of the perception, in other words, or they are realized or not. I understand that perhaps Freud did not talk about the feeling itself, but of the representations to him linked. They would be such emphasized, unconscious representations that would provoke superego judgment and the feeling of correlated blame.

In Inhibitions, Symptoms and Anguish, Freud (1926/1996), after having accomplished a profound reformulation in your theory of the mental operation, it tries to adjust old and new concepts, sometimes, not always successful. For Freud (1926/1996) the inhibitions necessarily do not have a pathologic character. A symptom denotes in fact the presence of some pathological process. The sexual function is responsible for a great number of disturbances that can classify it as simple inhibitions. The disturbances of the sexual function are caused by a great variety of reasons: The libido just can be diverted; The function cannot be so very exercised; It can be complicated by terms to her imposed, or modified by deviations for other ends; It can be impeded by measures of safety; If cannot be impeded of start, it can be immediately interrupted by the anguish appearance and, if however, it is completed, can come a subsequent reaction of protest and an attempt to undo what it was done. The nutrition function suffers a constant perturbation of an inclination to do not eat that occurs for a libido retracting. In some neurotic terms, the locomotion suffers an inhibition in the walking or a weakness in the walk. In the inhibition for the work, the patient feels a pleasure decrease in performs it or becomes capable of accomplished it well. The inhibitions are defined like resistances to the ego functions, imposed like measures of caution or occur as a result of an energy decrease. The ego adopts the mould inhibitions to avoid a conflict with the ID or with superego.

For Freud (1926/1996), a symptom is a signal and a substitute of a satisfaction impulse that remained temporarily inactive; It is a consequence of repression process. Repression proceeds of the ego when this refuses to associate itself with an investment impulse originated in the ID. The ego is capable, by means of repression, of prevent that the idea that serves of vehicle to the pulse becomes conscious. The ego is the anguish headquarters. The ego, in order to oppose a process impulsive of the ID just has that give a displeasure signal to obtain the principle pleasure help with the purpose of surpassing the ID. The ego also obtains its influence in view of their intimate connections with the conscience phenomenon. The ego removes the external and internal dangers for identical lines. As well as the ego controls the action line concerning the outer world, also controls the access to the conscience. In the emphasizes, it exercises its force in both the directions, acting of a way on the pulse and of other on the psychic representative of that pulse. Most regressions found at work therapeutic are cases of posterior pressure. A symptom arises of a impulse affected by the regression. The impulse expresses through a substitute who is reduced, dislocated and inhibited. This way, the ego can exercise control on the ID as well as to be up to him. The same it applies to superego. The ego, actually it is the part organized most of the ID. Usually for impulse that should be emphasized remains isolated. To the initial act of emphasizes it follows a tiring or endless sequence in which the fight against for drives it prolongs in a fight against the symptom. In this defensive fight the ego presents two facets with contradictory expressions.

A behavior line that adopts results that its own nature obliges it to do something that should be considered like a restoration or reconciliation attempt. The presence of a symptom can imply in a certain capacity prejudice, what can be used to calm down some exigency by superego or to refuse some demand of the outer world. Thus, the symptom gradually becomes the representative of important interests. In the obsessive neurosis and in the paranoia the forms that the symptoms take over become very valuable for the ego, because they get for him not some advantages but a satisfaction narcissist that, of other form, would not exist. All this results in a secondary benefit of the disease that is followed to the neurosis. The second behavior line adopted by the ego is less friendly, given it continues in the meaning of the emphasizes. In the little case Hans, for example, the boy refused to leave to the street for having that a horse bit it. It met in the jealous and hostile attitude of Oedipus for with the father, the who loved profoundly. Here the conflict it owed to the ambivalence: A much based love and a not less driven justifiable hatred to an only and same person. The little phobia Hans should have been an attempt to solve the conflict. The pulse that suffered emphasizes in the little

Hans was a hostile pulse against his father. Hans alleged be afraid of that a horse bit it. The idea of being devoured by the father is a tendered childhood material. This idea has parallels in the mythology and in the kingdom animal. The emphasizes attacked two impulses: A sadistic aggressiveness against the father and a tender and passive attitude regarding him. The formation of its phobia had the effect of abolishing totally the investment of object by your mother. The force motivator of the emphasizes was the fear of an imminent castration. Your fear of being bitten by a horse can have the meaning of a fear that the horse plucked his genital organs and castrated it. A phobias comparison presented by the Wolves Man and by the little Hans shows that, although there were striking differences in your cases, the result was the same. This we explain by the anguish exam of the two patients of Freud. It verified be the anguish a reaction to the fear of castration. It wants faced as real and immediate. It was this anguish that, when occurring in the ego, unchained the regression process that finally conducted to the phobia formation. The anguish proceeded having two fonts: One of the ID (libido disturbance) and to other of the ego (Freud, 1926/1996).

On the other hand, when Freud (1926/1996) observes what happens with the conversion hysteria, finds an anguish total absence. The symptoms formation in the conversion hysteria is to him obscure. It presents a multiple situation and varied without any viable explanation. The commonest symptoms in the conversion hysteria are the motive paralysis, contractures, the actions or involuntary discharges, pains and hallucinations. They constitute investment processes that can be permanent or intermittent. The relative symptoms to the obsessive neurosis, on the other hand, relapse in two groups, that present opposite tendencies. Or they are prohibitions, cautions and atonements, or they are substitutive satisfactions that appear with frequency under a symbolic disguise. Reinforcing the regression, the ego obtains its first success in the defensive fight against the libido exigencies. Perhaps is more in the obsessive cases that in the normal or hysterical that defense's force motivator is the castration complex and that that is being remote be Oedipus complex tendencies. The reactive formations in the ego of the obsessive neurotic should be faced like a defense's mechanism in excess. Other defense's mechanisms to what can cite in this situation are: The retroactive annulment the regression and the isolation. The ambivalence also contributes a lot for the formation of the obsessive neurosis, of unknown form. The main task during latent period seems to be the temptation dismissal of if masturbates. This fight produces a series of symptoms that appear under a typical form in the more different individuals and that, in general, present a ceremonial character. The puberty advent opens a decisive chapter in the history of the obsessive neurosis. Superego super-rigorous insists on sexuality repression. In the obsessive neurosis the conflict worsens in two directions the defensive forces become more intolerant than the forces to be avoided. Both effects they owe to the libido regression. There are obsessions in which the blame does not appear, or it is inexistent, because, somehow, these absence state of blame seem to be connected to the impulses satisfaction purely masochists.

There are two ego activities that form the symptoms and that deserve special attention for consist in regression substitutes. These activities are the annulment that it was done and the isolation. The first has a wide reach of application. It built a negative magic and makes an effort by means of the symbolism motor. For undoing not only the consequences of some event but also the event itself. In the obsessive neurosis, the technique of retroactive annulment than was done is first in the symptoms two fazes in which an action is cancelled by a second, so that everything if pass as if no action had occurred. This goal of the retroactive annulment is the second underlying reason of the obsessive ceremonials, being the first to take all the rational cautions of mould to prevent the occurrence or repetition of some particular event. The second technical, the isolation is peculiar to the obsessive neurosis. When something unpleasant occurs to the patient or when he himself did something that is important for its neurosis, it questions an interval during which nothing more should happen. It is especially difficult for the obsessive neurotic to execute the fundamental rule of the psychoanalysis. Your ego is more vigilant and do more drastic isolation, probably due to the tension high degree due to the conflict that there is between your superego and the ID. Making an effort itself to prevent thought associations and connections, the ego is obeying to one of the most old and fundamental orders of the obsessive neurosis: The taboo. Avoids it is of supreme importance in this disease because it is immediate goal of the investments of objects so much aggressive as loving (Freud, 1926/1996).

Freud (1926/1996) marks that in the phobias animals, the ego has to if you oppose to an investment of object libidinal that result from of the ID, investment this one that Pertence to Oedipus complex be positive or negative, because it believes that give way would imply him in the castration danger. The aggressive pulse results mostly of impulse of destruction. As soon as the ego recognizes the castration danger, gives an anguish signal and inhibits, through the pleasure-displeasure feeling the investment immediate process in the ID. Simultaneously, form itself the phobia. So, the castration anguish addressed an object and expresses of distorted way, so that the patient has fear do not be castrated by his father, but to of being bitten by a horse or devoured by a wolf. The phobias take over the projection character since they replace an internal danger impulse, for other external, perceptive. The anguish felt in the phobias animals is an affective reaction by the ego regarding the danger; the marked danger thus is the castration danger. A phobia generally establishes after a first anguish attack have been experienced in specific circumstances, such as in the street, in a train, in the plane, in the automobile or in the loneliness of a house. The anguish is a reaction to the danger situation. It is neutralized by the ego fact do something to avoid this situation or to run away from her. The symptoms, so, are sold like that created to avoid a danger situation whose presence was marked by the anguish appearance. The neurosises narcissistic are explained in terms of the existence of a sexual factor, the narcissism, which emphasizes the nature libidinal of auto preservation instinct. Since the unconscious cannot conceive its annihilation, and that should supply some contribution for the neurosises narcosis formation, then the fear of the death should be similar to the fear of the castration. The ego reacts against be abandoned by superego protective, to the destiny moulds. Moreover, the protective breastplate against excessive quantities of external excitation breaks.

In the continuity of your ideas, Freud (1926/1996) considers the anguish like an affective state and that its analysis reveals the existence of a specific characteristic of displeasure, discharge and perception acts of these acts. The anguish state is considered as a birth trauma reproduction. The anguish arises originally as a reaction to a danger state. It is reproduced whenever the danger state turns to occur. We only comprehend some few anguish manifestations in the children. They occur, for example, when the child is alone, or in the darkness, or when it is with a person ignored with which is not habituated. These three situations can be reduced to a unique condition: Miss of someone to who loves and for who craves for. The person's image mnemonics sweetheart is without a doubt intensely lunges, probably, at the beginning, of hallucinatory form. However, this does not produce the desired result and seems that desire it transforms in anguish. The economic disturbance caused by stimulus quantities accumulation needs to be eliminated. The dissatisfaction of an increasing tension owed to the need against which the child tries to protect itself repeats the birth danger situation. To depart of this point the anguish suffers several transformations parallels to the various development libidinal apprenticeships. The object loss importance as anguish determinant extends for a time's long period. The castration anguish, belonging to the phase phallica, also constitutes a fear of separation and, consequently, is linked to the same determinant. In this case, the danger is to of being separated of the genital organs. The transformation next is caused by superego forces. The castration anguish transforms in a moral anguish. Love loss performs the same role in the hysteria that the castration menaces in the phobias and the fear of superego in the obsessive neurosises. The anguish current concept belongs to a signal given by the mould ego to activate the pleasure-displeasure principle. There is no superego anguish or of the ID. The ID only can be the processes headquarters that take the ego to produce anguish.

It can say that for Freud (1926/1996), the symptoms formation and the anguish generation own two general focuses. One is the one of that the anguish constitutes, in herself, a neurosis symptom. The other is that there is an intimate relation between both. According to the second focus, the symptoms just form to avoid the anguish. The symptoms are maids of form to remove the ego of a danger situation. If the symptoms are impeded to form, the danger in fact materializes. The symptoms formation finishes with the danger situation. The defensive process is similar to the escape by means of which the ego removes of a danger that the exterior menace. The defensive process is an escape attempt of a danger impulse. The anguish determinants study shows the defensive behavior of the ego transfigured in a rational light. Each danger situation corresponds to a development life or phase particular period of the mental device. A great number of person remains infantile in her behavior concerning the danger and do not overcome the anguish determinants that were become obsolete. The vestiges of infantile neurosises can be detected in all the neurotic adults, however, neither all the children who show these signals become neurotic in the posterior life. Should occur therefore, that some anguish determinants be abandoned and some danger situations lose its meaning as the individual matures. Moreover, some theses danger situations manage to subsist until posterior times, modifying its determinants of mould anguish to updates them. Other anguish element, such like the fear of superego is destined to do not disappear.

As we saw the anguish is the reaction to a danger. If the ego manages to protect itself from a dangerous pulse through the process of emphasizes, I inhibited and it damages the part of the ID at issue; But at the same time gives to the ID some independence and renounces from part of its own sovereignty. Among factors that play a role in the neurosises cause and that create the terms under which are mind's forces enter shock excel three: A biological, a phylogenetic and a purely psychological. The biological factor is the time's long period during which a youth of the human species finds in an abandonment and dependence condition. The existence of the phylogenetic factor just it bases in inference. We were taken to presume its existence for a notable characteristic in the libido development. The man's sexual life does not do a constant progress of the birth to the maturity, but after an initial bloom until the fifth year, on an interruption. Afterwards its course in the puberty retakes the beginning interrupted in early life. The third factor, psychological, resides in a deficiency of our mental device that is related precisely with the differentiation between ID and ego and that, therefore, also can be attributed, in last resort, to the influence of the outer world. The ego cannot protect itself from internal dangers such as well as the derived of the external reality. It finishes accepting the symptoms formation in change of weakening drives (Freud, 1926/1996).

For Freud (1926/1996), an important element in the theory of the emphasizes is the opinion that this is not an event that occurs once, but that requires a permanent waste of energy. If this expense interrupted, the emphasized pulse that is adapting itself all time in its fonts, in occasion next would flow by the canals of which was expels and emphasizes it would fail in its purposes or would have to if repeat an indefinite number of times'. It is by the fact of drives belong to continuous nature that the ego has to assure its defensive action through a permanent waste. This action, undertaken to protect emphasizes it, can be observed in the analytic treatment under the resistance form. The resistance presupposes what it is called against-investment. Freud locates five types of resistances: The ego resistances, subdivided in regression resistances, of transfer and of secondary gain of the disease; the resistance of the ID, in other words, the compulsion to the repetition; Superego resistance, the feeling of blame or the need to punishment. The ego is the anguish source. The anguish is the general reaction at danger situations. The term defense is employed explicitly like a general designation of all the techniques of which the ego uses in the conflicts and that can take to the neurosis. The term emphasizes is private for a defense's special method. The defense's concept includes all the processes that have the same purpose, the ego protection against the exigencies drives (Freud, 1926/1996).

The anguish has an unequivocal relation with the expectation, it is anguish concerning about of something. It has a characteristic of indefinites and of object lack. In terms of more necessary, we use the word fear instead of anguish, if this has found an object. There are two reactions to the real danger. The first is an affective reaction, appearance of anguish. The other is a protective action. A danger situation is a recognized, abandonment reminded and waited situation. The anguish is the original reaction to the abandonment in the trauma and reproduces afterwards in the danger situation with a help request signal. The ego, that tried the trauma passively, now repeats it actively in a weak version, in the hope of being capable of alone to direct its own course. It seems to there is an intimate relation among anguish and neurosis; because the ego defends against a danger impulses through the anguish exactly like it does it against a real external danger. However, this line of defensive activity results eventually in a neurosis, due to an imperfection of the mental device (Freud, 1926/1996).

For Freud (1926/1996), in the anguish discussion, fear present and important in all your work and clinical thought, the child's situation who misses of its mother is not a danger situation, but yes a traumatic situation, since the child is feeling a need that would fit to the mother satisfy. It transforms in a danger situation if this is not present at the moment. The first anguish determinant, that the own ego introduces, is the object perception loss. Later, the experience teaches the child who the object can be present but angry with her. So, the object love loss becomes a new danger and determinant of much more lasting anguish. The suffering is the real reaction to the loss of an object while the anguish is the reaction to the danger that the loss causes. The suffering occurs, in the first childhood, like something regular, whenever a stimulus that is imposed about the periphery breaks the protective devices against the stimulus and prosecutes to act like a permanent stimulus, against which the muscular action, that is efficient because it protects the location that suffers the action from stimulus, finds impotent. When there is physical pain, it occurs a high degree that it can be denominated investment narcissistic of the sore location. This investment continues to increase and tends to deflate the ego. The transition of the physical pain for the mental pain corresponds to an investment narcissistic change for the object investment. The mourning occurs under the reality test influences, as we will see ahead in the depression study, because this function asks categorically that the patient separates of the object, given it does not exist most. The mourning is task warden of making this object dismissal in all situations in which it occurred an investment high degree.

With a good theoretical construction accomplished until years' final 30 last century, Freud (1939/1996) already could answer what if it wait for of the psychoanalysis while therapeutic technique. There are three decisive factors for the success or failure of the analytic treatment: The traumas influence, the constitutional force of drives, and the ego alterations. The constitutional factor belongs to decisive importance right from the start. However, a drive reinforcement that occurs in a posterior period of life can cause the same effects. In two occasions during the individual, right development drives suffer a considerable reinforcement: Puberty and, in the women's case, in the menopause. Do not surprise us if a person who was never neurotic, thus becomes in these times. Making an effort itself to replace repression insecure by controls ego reliable, not always we reach our goal in all its extension. We manage to make the transformation but with frequency just partially. The analysis not always it manages to guarantee in enough degree the foundations about which ones bases drive control. The cause of this partial failure is easily discovered. In the past, the quantitative factor of the force of drive to the defensive efforts of the ego was opposed; by this reason sought the psychoanalysis help; Nowadays the same factor establishes a limit to the effectiveness of this new effort. If drive force is excessive, the matured ego, sustained by the analysis, does not manage to accomplish its task, exactly like the defenseless ego failed previously.

In the that say respect to the analytic prophylaxis against conflicts impulsive, Freud (1939/1996) suggests that just two only methods can be taken in consideration: 1) The artificial production of new conflicts through the transfer (conflicts that do not own characteristics of reality), and 2) the appearance of these conflicts in the patient's imagination talking about them and turning it familiarized with the possibility that they occur. Revealing to the patient the possibilities of other conflicts impulsive, raise in it the expectation that these conflicts can occur. What wait is that this information and warning have the effect of activating in the patient one of the conflicts in a conservative rank but enough for the treatment. The expected result does not occur; everything that did was to increase its knowledge without anything change in it. In fact, the decisive factors for the success of the therapeutic efforts are the influence of the traumatic etiology, the relative force of drives that have of being controlled, and an ego alteration. The analytic situation consists in ally us to the patient's ego under treatment, of mould to subdue parts of the ID that are not under control. The ego has to try to accomplish its mediator task between ID and the outer world, for pleasure principle service and to protect the ID from dangers of the outer world. Under the education influence, the ego gets used to removing the exterior fight stage for the interior and to dominate the internal danger before it becomes external. During its fight in the two fronts, the ego does several methods use to accomplish its task, that is to avoid the danger, the anguish and the displeasure. These methods are called defense's mechanisms. In the psychoanalysis, the defense's mechanisms driven against the previous danger resurge in the treatment method like resistance against the cure. This way, the ego treatment the cure like a new danger. The therapeutic effect depends on turn the conscious that is emphasized in the ID. The effect caused in the ego by the defenses can be described how an ego alteration, if for this reason we understand a deviation of the normal ego that would guarantee an unshaken loyalty to the analysis work. The result of an analytic treatment depends essentially of the force and depth these resistances that cause an ego alteration.

Each ego is endowed of dispositions and individual tendencies. The properties than we come across us under resistance form can be determined by the heredity or acquired in defensive fights. There are several kinds of resistance.

There are people to who attributes a special tenacity of the libido. Other group of patient takes over an attitude that can be attributed to a depletion of the plasticity, of the alterations and larger development capacity. In a group of cases, the distinctive characteristics of the ego, that they can be considered as resistances sources against the analytic treatment and impediment to the therapeutic success, they can come of different and more profound roots. In this case work with the primordial facts that the psychological research can study: The behavior of the two drives primary, its distribution, coalition and separation. When studying the phenomena that prove the destruction drive activity, do not limit us to the observations of the pathologic material. Always there were but also there are people who can take as sexual goals members of his own sex as much as the of the opposite sex, without a tendency interferes with to another. Both Empedocles' fundamental principles are the even though Eros and Destruction: The first makes an effort in combine all that there is in every time larger units, while the as it makes an effort for them (Freud, 1939/1996).

Freud (1939/1996) points that in 1927, Ferenczi administered an instructive conference about the analysis terminus problem. It finishes with for affirmation refreshing that the analysis is not an endless process, but I yes prosecute that it can arrive to a natural end with enough ability and patient by the analyst. Ferenczi take it like another point important the success fact depend a lot of the analyst have learnt a lot with his mistakes and equivocal, as well as have overcome the weakest points of its personality. It is unquestionable that the analysts itself in his personality did not reach invariably the standard of psychic normality which wish infusing in their patients. The psychoanalysis opponents frequently point this fact with gibe and use it like argument at show the uselessness of the analytic efforts. The special terms of the analytic work really make the defects of the analyst interfere in a patient state correct evaluation preventing an useful reaction to them. The terminus of an analysis is a practical subject. All experienced analyst is able to recall countless cases in which it fired definitively of the patient. The analysis purpose is to assure the best possible psychological terms to the ego operation.

So much in the therapeutic analysis as in the character analysis, they arise two prominent themes that cause extraordinary difficulties to the analyst: The penis envy, one desire defined of the woman to own a masculine genital organ and, in the man, a fight against the passive or feminine attitude regarding other man. What is common to two themes was denominated like an attitude driven to the castration complex. In both cases, the attitude for with the opposite sex succumbed to the emphasizes. The supreme importance of these two subjects did not pass unnoticed Ferenczi. In the conference by he pronounced in 1927, it postulated like exigencies for the successful analyses that these two complexes had been dominated. In no other aspect of the analytic work suffers more than one oppressive sensation that all the efforts went in vain than when it is trying to persuade a woman to abandon her wish to own a penis, for being impossible, or when it tries to convince a man that a passive attitude regarding other men not always it means castration and is indispensable in many life relations. For man's super compensation rebellious produce one of the most strong resistances transferer. The resistance prevents that it occurs any alteration in its personality (Freud, 1939/1996).

Chapter 2
Psychoanalytical Field

2.1. Psychoanalytical Field: An approach

Until the present moment, we talk about the speech contrary, of the possible meanings that in it are recorded and of the interpretation possibilities, without however, thus hope, have lost the initial goal of clarify the rule that enables the analytic game.

We can think, and not at random, that there should be some principle ordered that raise and guides the material choice that is presented and that propitiates the interpretation. If we play a net at the sea, by the thickness and greatness will give to if it have a fishes size slight idea that we are aiming; However, only after you to pull out of water is that are going to have the certainty of the caught species and, thence, the inopportune shoals that are not us interesting will be launched again to the sea, alive or dead.

In spite of everything, that is, of the not seized fishes, the launched net seems to be a basic point of ordination for a good fishery. Clear, when the sea is for fish!

By the fact of not being fishermen and neither we walk equipped with nets, do not fail to "fish" forms of being that they are submerged, that swim in the profundities of the soul of that that in our front lays down to if "fish". Some principle ordered and orienting, as well as in the fishing, there should be before for infiniteness of possible heartfelt that remits to talks about the analyzing. Well, if there are not, who knows how to we will be, in a determined moment, "fishing with a holed our net floating attention, liberate and selective, if is not very forced to tell, it can have, for analogy, some likeness with the net play to the sea that, through their buoys, even submerged, semifloatin to the sea waves flavor. Meanwhile, what if raisin with the net and the fishes is a submerged dance, nothing interesting or special, until a big shoal and of good weight makes feel its weight. Again, and forcing a certain analogy, something also we impose to our net, that is, to our free, floating and selective attention. For the ones that are an expert in fishing, apologize me because actually I was never fisherman; of this other "fishery", whereby if note, am a mere apprentice, that many and many times plays the improper net and, or, even holed.

But the fishes order by themselves in front of the net and, it fits to the fishermen select what them interesting, how for our side, the of the psychoanalysis, the analyst gathers what it offers him and guides yourself by the psychoanalytical theory, that is going to indicate that that is going to be more important to the emotional configurations of a patient in particular. Maybe so much in the fishery case as in the of the analysis, both the terms do not perform the requisites that can give keep an account of our original inquiry, that is, which ones among multiple felt of the patient speech owe or deserve to be chosen and as if give such selection.

In the fishery case, nothing indicates that by the net size and resistance would have, by her only, big fishes - what we theoretically foresee, since previous experiences, other fisheries, indicate the need to a thick and strong net, but the net does not determine the fish. In the analysis, the matter of the natural selection does not formalize as a convincing answer and, less yet, that the important, correct meanings, would impose. Imagine, only the big fishes fighting to be caught by the net! On the other hand, the theory does not fail to be the collection and organization of the thought they made in the practice that for signal is exclusively dependent of a certain selective work to do not become a theoretical lie, disentailed of any situation that could be contemplated. A net more than holed, if it thus was.

Letting the fishery aside, I think she contributed in the that it could to bring to our "net" two concepts that will be able to show itself as the determinants, possible meanings organizers and indicators that are presented and that without them patient's associations would take the way to the infinite. I talk about the unconscious and transfer concepts.

We find in Herrmann (1991, p.87) that: "The idea of a spontaneous selection of material to interpret has certain base; That is, that we verify, in the clinic, there be an attraction polo for listens her analytic, constituted by the coherence of some sense organizations (unconscious) and one saw which he attracts our attention (transfer). 'If we remind of the classical form as Freud interpreted the dreams, dividing the dream manifest into extracts, isolated parts, and asking so that everything that occurred to the mind, without exception, was communication, the emerging associations went, successively, converging to determined points and, finally, earned meaning and order, unveiling the latent oneiric thoughts. For this associations virtual convergence area can, without forcing so much the situation, call unconscious: Processes of before hidden thoughts and loaded of affection, to the which ones arrives, for example, after the analysis terminus of a dream any that is put to the interpretation. The interesting in this proposed interpretative model by Freud is that the interpretation and latent content, that is, the unconscious, coincide and, if thus the is, only remains us can talk about unconscious like interpretation brother twin-Siamese, because the psychoanalytical unconscious express the subject emotions internal order, while the transfer is a kind of emotional vector that guides for the analyst the repetition of basic standards of the feel, reevaluate.

So, the unconscious would be, thus, the convergence intrapsychic point, the internal order of the emotions and the transfer, emotional vector - driven to the analyst - of the pregnant contents of emotions that in a determined presents moment were done.

This way, unconscious and transfer compose the selective net that is established from the talk about the analyzing and of the listens of the analyst, heartfelt unveiled in one way of the patient action in the field transfer, by the interpretation, that "fishing" what should be fish, because the meanings that were organized and that proceeded making sense, occurred in a determined instant specify of the established relation. As if to for any thought, of any content that at that moment was found by the interpretation, he certainly, will be replete of emotion, and the emotion as human quality of the higher importance, will deserve a highlight anything negligible in the psychoanalysis. It fits to the psychoanalysis, for vocation; unveil its logic, the unconscious, its internal matrix organizer. The emotion is of extreme importance with regard to the therapeutic effectiveness, and the representations that pulsing front to the conscience in condition to analysis, will be caught, defended or expurgated in syntony with its emotional value. It does not conceive perception that is not emotional, the more those than we can glimpse in we ourselves.

Approaching at every turn of a central concept up to now persecuted and letting matters we answered, not only whereby up to now our discoveries reveal us, Campo Psychoanalytical goes showing itself like a rule and human being's special condition where the conscience it apprehends to herself, not by reflection, but by means of simultaneous differences with himself own, of alternative representations that break the field of effective reputed representation. In the dreams field, the latent content found by the interpretation can be an enlightening example of the differences, of the alternative representations in which it comes across the conscience in condition to analysis. The analysis without that that is you peculiar can be an activity that is restricted the only a faces reading, a statics exercise engineered facial by the routine and consensual talk; However, it can thus never accomplish its vocation, the one of unveil the soul features. Because of this, Field's Psychoanalytical notion goes successively earning importance, for perhaps being the demanded essence.

Running the risk of being repetitive, I find necessary to countersign, once again any ideas that will go showing itself extremely useful to our purpose, that is, apprehend Field's Psychoanalytical concept, the "rule" that enables the analytic game, for analogy to the rule of the cards game. For that, and with a little more of patience, think it would be convenient, for sometimes, detain us in the fantasy concept and of how the interpretation can, during a session and of the future sessions that the analytic process floodgate, have some expressive value that corresponds to that of her waits: An interpretation that presents and add an alternative representation to the repertoire already fastened by the patient.

There is the possibility to take the expression fantasy under several aspects, under several shade of color that connote her. In the everyday, in the daily talk, referent us to the fantasy when it presents us how a tale, a fantastic communication that, for vice or automatism, contrast what it is us communication with immediate experience, with the reality and with a certain relations logics evaluation established in the text itself, its content and its referring, as well as the own subject.

It is not alone characteristic of daily talk; it makes part of the psychiatric diagnosis that is served of these relations, of this connotation given to the expression fantasy with much more rigidity.

In the psychoanalysis also find several connotations for this expression, I detain me here to only a small part, because its utilization belongs to very widespread use, and would give, certainly another dissertation's Master. Among possible uses have: "Imaginary staging in which the individual is present and that illustration, in a manner more or less deformed by the defensive processes, the accomplishment of one wish and, in last analysis, of one wish unconscious" [...] "The ghost or fantasy it presents under several modalities: Conscious fantasies or diurnal dreams; Unconscious fantasies - such as the analysis reveals how underlying structures to a content manifest: Proto fantasies" (Laplanche & Pontalis, 1983, p.228)

They point Laplanche and Pontalis, in the cited work that "we are taken to define ghost (fantasy) like a production purely illusory that would not resist to a correct apprehension of the real Moreover, some Freud's Texts seem to justify this orientation. In *Formulations on both Principles of the Psychic Operation* (1911/1990), Freud opposes to the interior world, which tends towards the satisfaction by the illusion, an outer world than imposes progressively to the individual, through the "perceptive system, the reality principle.

However, without denying such concepts, the expression fantasy, for Herrmann, does not mean an absurd communication, or that should be searched in the depths of the mind, or still something that should suffer or to have as contrast the reality, specifically when such expression refers to the context of a session. In such context, it would be a way to if listen without particular preference, all the words, all the communications that a patient pronounces and that denote felt another, vector indicate directed to who listens, to the analyst, established specific field, where such expressions take reason of being, that is, in the transfer.

Thence, the fantasy life does not show reason any to be demanded in an antagonistic psychic activity that produce and organize the articulated, conscious speech, of the reason. What we put is that the words connotative possibilities indetermination has for consequence the production of heartfelt other that accompany *I gave birth* pass talk it goal. The speech, the word, how already I pointed previously, by its double function of creating in the present situation and of communicating, failure: Communicating much less that it was created; it fecundates the interpretative possibilities, since all communication presents as discovery possibility. Everything, this way, it shows like fantasy. The fantasy puts, so, like the "reality" unique of the analysis.

If we think of speech meanings indetermination, of the words that compose it with its characteristic of equivocate, the fantasy guarantees the interpretative possibilities, remaining investigate as if it organizes an interpretation and can give it to quality validation of true or false. When we think of patient's speech, the material, the meanings that of him loosen, they cross and they uncross. For this intersection will go forming meanings that taking its respective importance for listens her of the analyst, liberate and selective. Such meanings given birth by such listens they reveal in the speech express of the analyst, thought of the interpretation. The interpretation, this way, it puts like the organization, convergence of the countless meanings of the speech, that for its side, not hiding its origin, it reveals like another optional fantasy the one that is being interpreted.

After the interpretation is pronounced, the patient's associations for it directional, continue, they modify, take other shade of color that will enable, by the same previous condition, a new interpretation. However, the interpretations will go being included in a series that point a meaning unification of all the included interpretations in this series. The series is sketched not from the material next to an interpretation, but by the material interpretation next; we otherwise would have how answers to a specific set of associations that would not enable any convergence of meanings among them, a ping pong game.

"In satisfactory terms of the analytic process, they occur interpretations series more and more including keeping to each other a coherence relation [...] lacking a common meaning to interpretations, or such meaning being so material wide and distant, that this last to proceeds being it indifferent" (Herrmann, 1991, p.99).

This way, an isolated interpretation, by itself, disconnected of an interpretative series will vacate to aimless, uncertain and without any value that corresponds to its function, that is, propitiate, more and more, wider, more including knowledge of this patient, enlarging its capacity and psychic mobility of represent itself and the reality, as well as the truths of himself that were being joined and that were have meanings. From this done, the veracity is function relational of the interpretations, in the analytic process, just it supports in the fantasies, in the equivocal meanings that put on view, with character of possible and at the moment in which it is pronounced (Herrmann, 1991).

2.2. Field and Fields' Rupture

For Herrmann (1991, p.105), "the field is everything and anything in the relation; It is the order producer of heartfelt but is not any meaning in particular; It guides the concrete productions, but does not own any syncretistic."

In the analysis, the patient communicates, even when it is in silence or relates a situation, it comments things that relate to him etc., establishing a communication field, and it hopes that your analyst follows it, like in any talks rational, in the field by him proposed.

However, when the analyst interprets, evidences what it was proposed by the patient, but in an other field, causing strangeness, indignation and so many other emotional reactions that such communication can to that patient raise. Actually, another field by the interpretation is suggested, propose, whose ticket does not give without anguish, frustration and, when finally in it comes in, that new field proceeds organizing the new communications, that again allow the field be broken. The field successive ruptures allow to the patient have sentiments other by the analyst and, above all, the possibility to see itself where never was seen, of earn what always had but of right never owned, a repertoire enlarged of himself, the possibility to modify yourselves.

Field Psychoanalytical, condition of being of the Psychoanalysis, can be defined, for approach, by the rupture possibility of the entire field that in it comes to happen. This way, it is impossible to of being appropriated by greater than be the effort, rule that enables the analytic game, where all the presents possibilities are done.

It listens her analytic, and does not matter where hears, that is, not just and exclusively in the surgery, seems to liberate itself of presupposing determinants, it puts back your free and selective attention in the emotional details, in the images that the communication goes forming, in the apparent changes of theme, trying to find a common region, where the interpretation expresses as the multiple contents organization, thought of several levels before having the manifest form.

An example of this situation, sometimes imponderable to who speaks and "see" what it was told in a way distorted, could be extracted of my work as psychologist in a São Paulo's Hospital. Report only a fragment: A patient twenty-five year, virus carrier HIV there is more than three years, was put into hospital in one of the floor infirmaries in which work for treatment of an opportunistic infection. After initial interview, I proceeded attending her twice a week. Very beautiful, physically very preserved, without any signal of being HIV's Carrier, it showed sociable and expressed much happiness when of my arrival. "Wow, how long, Hein! "We had week combined schedule and days, that is, she knew when we would go find. Since our first meeting, like in the posterior, talked about her life with much unknot. Parent's daughter separated since the five years old did not remind of any suffering so much by her mother, like her, that it could have been motivated by the separation, because, according to her, her mother was a very strong woman. Soon it lost the interest by the studies, in spite of presenting a very good vocabulary, of express she adequately and of having a general aspect very well care. It ran away from home still pre-teenager and to it immediately involved with drugs; it lived in a good house, of high average class, however, preferred to street. It smelt cocaine, it smoked marijuana. Her mother had tried of everything, since your father removed itself totally of his life, only had news through the grandmother; He felt well, I was what it knew. Among its mother's several attempts to recovers her, it told me some tickets, like Recovery House for Drugged, Therapeutic and Psychiatric Clinical Community. But anything advanced. A day, lasts, without a cents in the pocket, it came in an of these massage houses for men and ran for a place. It was immediately admitted. It talked about her career and of the facts of your life without any emotion, did not tell prostitute, but yes masseur. It seemed that anything reached you, not even HIV, was in hospital only for a throat treatment and as soon as had certificate of discharge from hospital, it would immediately come back to the work, after all, earned very well and not time to waste, needed a money.

"On the other side of her mother, perhaps you have meaning your parents' separation and, mostly, his of you. A fragile little girl, that saw totally abandoned and to for being the most drastic than it could have her occurred, nothing more could reach her, the worst already had happened. How you should feel cruel that your father just like at least it comes to pay a visit to the sick daughter, despite all the previous appeals. Already it does so much time, no".

It lowered the eyes for some instants as if it was to cry, however, lifted the head with an apparently tranquil smile, but her voice waves connoted the state of her spirit. "I asked talk to you and neither I know right why, but I think you should not pay attention to that I talk, think it is not worthwhile, my father does not come back anymore".

Starting from then it started to talk about your preoccupation, of the Aids and of the cautions that would have to take to do not infect other people, your clients, as it denominated the people who searched her services. I think she there was meaning have me infected with the history of her abandonment and of the sadness that had transformed your life, sorrow that loaded in the "suitcase" of her indifference.

It is such it listens without focus, "desolate" and to without aiming any target in particular to what enables the breaking of a certain field communicational, that we articulate and engineers from the transfer phenomenon. This, in the analytic situation, joy of a certain value disposition, where the said things establish partners' dialog positions. Such value disposition "enables a speech possible meanings filtration, to select the dimension of those that designate relative emotional places for patient and analyst, in given moment" (Herrmann, 1991, p.36).

What could be me representing at that specific moment for this patient? Who know your father, that thus if represent to hear how its life had become sad, disturbed by her abandonment. And when I remind me of your expression as soon as I arrived, always very willing, never of bad humor, always solicitous, would not be I, for consequence also representing your clients and, would not it be your paternal clients representatives? All these possibilities if represent in the field in which was it?

It is in the field transference that is born the "psychoanalytical man" that, by nature of the field that conceives it, is going to be marked by an identity constant crisis. In this field, the of the transfer, the analyst, among countless aspects and hue of the speech, captivates a general meaning and organizer and, when it expresses that other meaning in your communication, presents a new fantasy, alternative, that if shocks, mixture itself to the previous, playing the partners in a new field that is opened, where partners' emotional places again metamorphose.

For consequence of field that will be ed breaking and opening the possibility of other of them form, the patient does not manage to keep his habitual way of work with his representations, because, the each field breaking, the representation of yourself and of your reality goes being put in check. The wait of a new representation that redefines it, that puts back it in safe terrain is denominated by Herrmann of **transit expectation**, that is, hopes her that is given on the transit of a lost representation temporarily for another. Such transformations representational in the field of transference, they enable to the patient and to the analyst are where never thought, of experienced an emotions universe that give and colors an analytic process, a rich emotional adventure that is not exhausted.

By the qualities intrinsic of the field rupture operation, other forms of representing will go postulating itself. What we take, at least, is the universe representational enlargement, the escape of the representations exclude fasts and of hardening mental, and the possibility of psychic change that are opened as alternative.

There is a situation a little more drastic" of the described in the transit expectation, where multiple representations manage around without it can momentarily grab them, where the vertigo sensation, of absolute loss of him present is done. Herrmann denominates her of Vortex, that is, a whirl in which we fell and, to whom for him already passed; the only thing descriptively is the feeling, the anguish of being going mad. Not even they remain words, be them which ones are, in which it can grab.

What would cause that to unchain of the representations?

Herrmann points the analysis revelation that, concisely, would be when the analyst hit in the that saw and much more still in the that did not see, shooting the patient in an empty representational, in direction to the psychoanalytical field. This, as we saw, joy of a certain extravagance when guarantying the ruptures possibility of other field that in it happen being everything and, at the same time, nothing. The patient, under the effect vortex, falls into a precipice, imagine, reflected of representations, without caning hold yourself to none; I think the effect vortex can perhaps be imagined like a profound unsteadiness between essence and the appearance, the not represented drawing, or yet, a portrait without image.

I remind me of something like that have if past with me. It was soon after the year's end vacation, do not know if at the beginning, half or session end for signal, what had been told by the analyst did not seem to me anything of overtime, since I had ear things worse. There you have that suddenly the heart shoots, a dizziness sensation, of vertigo, profound and panting breathing, and a sudden wish of lifting me and of going away. I remained, do not know as. It did not find words to pronounce, they arrived until the language and did not leave, besides an endless series of thoughts that were happened quickly, but to without managing to detain me in any. When I heard analyst's voice signaling the session end, soon sat down in the couch, however the dizziness sensation lasted for more some instants. Just when I arrived to the door managed to concatenate something: "Today the thing was angry". The comments, crazy sensation report and of indisposition just gave on the session next and with much fear that such "anguish attack" returned to be repeated.

Psychopathic nuclei, catastrophic change, transitory symptoms etc., think they are good ways to if describe the effect vortex, constituent part of the analytic process.

2.3. The Rupture in the "flesh"

Why to awake me, oh spring breeze? You me acariasis *and speaks: "I spill on you the celestial drops of the dew! But it approaches time in which I will wither: It approaches the tempest that will pluck me the leaves! Tomorrow it will come the walker, it will come the one that saw me in full beauty: Your eyes; Search me for all camping and will not find me anymore!*

(Werther - J.W.Goethe)

Everybody went and they came back hurried, with smart, alive looks, from whom do not have time to waste, marking their footprints in the ground, through one tread firm, mark from whom knows what to do. Conversations in the aisle: Medical, nurses, auxiliaries of nursing, attendants. Also think it was in a hurry, I had patients to see, demands of one hospital floor. Suddenly, in the corner, specifically in an of these enclosures nicknamed of little pigsty, there was that imperceptible child: A little boy two year and some months, extremely thin, skin and bone, with scaling that covered you the skin and wounds dispersed by the whole body. To the side, a children's group sat down around of a small little table scribbled paper leaves with pencil by heart: To the top, sustained by a support, a connected television: "Xou" da Xuxa.

Everything we suddenly disconnected! Television, medical, paper, nurse, child, my badge in the breast. I found those eyes shining, lost in the infinite: Dreaming, who knows! A strangeness running through me of the feet to the head, a knot in the throat and in the breast and a silent action mine rhythm steps, my speech and my ears. I sit down, awkward know there as, in a little bench to the side. Lost my eyes were in those brilliant, fixed and profound eyes. They seemed to roam in a tunnel of thick and darkness walls; I think I as well, in that instant, was my search. During such approach the hospital actions lost its connection, its "logic"; of my ears moved away the sounds: I remind me just that I lowered the head and looked at the badge where, of tip-head, with my photo was read: Psychologist. Speechless, I caught me touched.

The thin little hand, the fingers with the nails extremities infected by streptococcus, slowly was showing me a paper sheet in white, pointing me a pencil. Approaching the pencil chosen at random among so many another, said him "is green". Grabbing the pencil with delicacy, approached the leaf adapting its tip between thumb and the index finger and sketched some scribbles that hardly impregnated the leaf of the green color. "What a pretty!" Said him. Without looking me continued to scribble, fine traces, almost imperceptible, that he sighing successively pointed me, slowly. At that moment, for me, the most beautiful traces than life force could let. It performed all leaf, stopped, looked me leisurely, turned the leaf, and pointed it with the pencil. "Yes, it is in white", said him. Tired, it released the pencil slowly, letting for me, the clear, profound notion that he owned of himself. The brilliant eyes loosened of the paper and went again for the infinite. Suddenly the knots of the breast and of the throat went, the muddy eyes clarified and the sound returned slowly to my ears. The psychologist, caricaturist by the badge, lost itself to whether find again in a human experience that little or almost nothing manage to relate, but that left the impression of a profound wisdom, found in a child two year and some months, where life, in his last whispers, it showed present with his creation power. In a simple scribble, imperceptible for the nurses and doctors that routinely cross that look brilliant in the infinite – "a patient little terminal", as it expressed affectionately a young doctor – found life that sprouted with all its wisdom. In the routine of a hospital, heartfelt are consensual remote, remaining only references established: "Patient little terminal". Field diary registration, I think it was broken. Besides another... It would be interesting to point out that I came having, until the present moment, many doubts regarding the continuity of my work in the hospitable institution, for signal, specialized in diseases infectious disease. Such doubts were arising of a certain self consideration that is, realized that my mental continent was not available for a patients' certain population: Disgusts, repugnance and presents fear were done. They influenced all relation, letting the psychological assistance in a strictly formal platform, a caricature that should be. It heard without listening, it realized me distant and little or almost nothing associated regarding the dialog contents kept with the patients. Theme of my own analysis, certainly.

However, after such experience, where the psychologist stayed of tip-head, I noticed that the disgust field, of the repugnance and of the fear broke, letting me the mental and affective freedom to approach contents other and to open me for so many other psychic realities that even then, defensively, kept me distant and dissociated. The presents associations were done and my interpretative capacity as well. Crisis moment and of impasse, the experience did me learn to represent me professionally in a way much more rich and enlarged.

The routine field checks meanings absorbed of emotion. All and any relation establishes a field, that if exhibition by its contrary.

2.4. Unconscious: Some consideration

Practically all the psychoanalysis schools postulate, one way or another, the existence of an unconscious. Some they inspire in the first topic, another, in the second, other yet, so much in the first as in the second. In short, the question of the unconscious has life in the psychoanalysis, multiple forms, and several incarnations.

However, when we pass in covers the texts by Fabio Herrmann, with rare exceptions, find references, for example, to Oedipus complex, to the ID, Ego, Superego, to the castration, that inhabit the unconscious, as well as impulses of life and of death and, not infrequent, feel the strangeness of being entering an unknown terrain, in an other field.

I remind me, in the quality of example, of a friend, that for signal had already running through a good course of your formation in psychoanalysis and, for a certain my person's influence, started to read the "Real". According he, lost the ground that sustained him, because all the reference well-known, the own jargon of our science seemed to have been subtracted and, this way, in almost nothing could hold himself, being the text, therefore and for your inherent complexity, almost impossible to of being comprehended by him at that moment. With little mistake margin, my friend was not the unique: myself, after several readings, many times abandon the text without owed her comprehension, when not, realize that the understanding that had had I was very fleeting, it disappears of the memory.

It would be the psychoanalysis vocabulary lack, of the established concepts, what would propitiate this unfamiliarity sensation and the comprehension difficulty? Or it would be already the unfamiliarity a text effect, field rupture, for example, where the customary representation of the texts what care for the psychoanalysis would be put in check, where a new representation puts like alternative, do it play thus the reader in a state (called by Herrmann) of **transit expectation**?

Questions somewhat difficult to are answered, since, to if it be sure, should test multiple variables, such as, write the texts with the established concepts and the notions that the same tries do us apprehend. Or search in the Herrmann's Work what could distinguish it from the Psychoanalysis foundations, for thence think the unfamiliarity is reasonable, for being itself of a new conception that anything has to see with the psychoanalysis. And, thence, yes, would be the author risking his psychoanalytical work that garating your money for pay the psychoanalytical bread each day, points like himself in the last part of the *Psychoanalysis Method: Real arrangements.*

Prosecute a little more.

Until there are very little time ago, the psychoanalysts and the psychoanalysis tried if differentiate of other therapeutic practices and of other theoretical formulations postulating any principles orderers and distinguishing; I do not remind of all, just would like to cite some. First, the acceptance of the infantile sexuality, principle this absorbed and accepted not only for other existing lines in the psychology, but also accepted in a way so fast by the occidental society that carries us to suspect of how for Victorian morale was pilfered to continue surviving. sexy itself everything and, by the generalization, the sexuality was without sexy itself, where, soon, will be all of us again asking what it after all has to see coitus with sexuality.

I intend to tell that the simple acceptance of the infantile sexuality and the one of the adult man, by its inherent banality, does not show today enough – whether is just that was a day – to turn accepts any practice or theory like psychoanalytical. Reich who tell it!

A second principle and perhaps the most important, it would be in the division acceptance of the psychic personality between conscious and unconscious, or better telling, the existence acceptance of the unconscious.

I think many other could still be cited, like impulses theory, the transfer and for contra-transfer. However, I think of detain me in this point, that is, the of the existence acceptance of the unconscious in the determination of our psychic life.

I think, even for Freud, the matter of the unconscious was of the more important, and if everything started with him, remember.

The unconscious Freudian, in summaries, would be constituted by the traces inherited of the genetics, that would bring the registration from the experiences of our own phylogenies, as well as by the repressed, being the unconscious repressed, but the unconscious being much more that the repressed. Like adjective, the unconscious term is nominated in your work to denote contents that are not present in the conscience in a determined moment, as well as, the same term, unconscious is used to do a certain differentiation topic, like one of the systems that would have the access of its contents barred by repression to the system pre-conscious-conscious. In the Second topic, we have the ID like original instance of the psyche, its instinctive substratum; their contents are the psychic representatives of impulses. When being born, the individual would be pure ID that, progressively, due the reality exigencies, in its periphery, goes forming itself another differentiated instance, that is, the ego. The ego, it would embrace the system pre-conscious-conscience and to for being a layer derivative of the ID, does not fail to own good part of itself unconscious, thus with several characteristics of its operation.

To other instance of this representation of the proposed mental device by Freud, superego, also is a differentiated part, only that of the ego.

Superego formation gives for consequence of Oedipus complex decline, when the child renounces from satisfaction of her wishes oedipal targets of the prohibition and transforms its investments libidinous in identification. Superego, for Freud, dives profoundly in the ID, demarcating this way, its fundamental form of operation, that is, unconscious.

As we notice, in this small summarize, the quality of being of the unconscious keeps its substance in the theory Freudian and does not lose its importance for the understanding of the pertaining to the soul life.

Well, and by Herrmann?

By Herrmann, on the other hand, there is not an unconscious located in any mind's region. What for he there are unconscious multiple – to be more faithful its terminology, relative unconscious: For each relation, a field as presupposed organizer. The rupture of this specific field – the relative unconscious makes the field pass to the relation. This way, the unconscious "does not exist", however, "there is".

Its there be is in the relation dependence, of the field and of its breaking, and, only after the field breaking, they reveal their presuppose organizers, that is, the unconscious.

On the other hand, whether we think of unconscious Freudian soon will realize that there are things in the unconscious that never will be able to be or to have conscious representation, how, for example, the phylogenetic inheritance, metabolism processes results and good part of the repressed. Of such things, for Herrmann, nothing will be able to talk, unless are unconscious. Trying to think inside the parameters postulated by Herrmann, would perhaps be relations which field organizer never could be broken and, this way, is not possible to organize any representation.

Would he have the proposed unconscious by Herrmann some mail with some of the models Freudian?

See what he himself tells us, to see it is possible some comparison: If be it to the conscience is to be conscious, the being of the unconscious is to be possible conscience, in the scope of the interpretative operations.

Is not due to, this way, to incur in the vulgar mistake of consider the sentence that capture the unconscious in an interpretation as index of a concrete entity, discovered for cost and by little palpate. The entity it exhausts in the expression and does not overtake the analytic moment that expressed her, it has by way of being the interpretation.

Only the interpretation is worth, for the Psychoanalysis, like knowledge methodologically source specific. Being the unconscious only an interpreted, operational fault value to any affirmation about this one that does not start and finish in the interpretation (Herrmann, 1991, p.331)

Soon at the beginning of the citation notice the proposition definitive of the unconscious for Herrmann, as well as, can, without forcing very the circumstances, establish your relation and likeness with some part of the model Freudian. Be possible conscience, means, in my opinion, the unconscious that can become conscious, that is, it pre-conscious Freudian that, descriptively, are contents that have the access possibility to the conscience, I mean, of being possible conscience.

Thence, so, can think all proposed operation by Herrmann, that is, the system field-relation and of the field rupture would give exclusively in the systems pre-conscious-conscious limits, not saying and, by consequence, also could not deny anything that postulates any other possibility that was put out of such limits.

Herrmann countersigns itself in our part understanding when it postulates that meta psychology the belief would be a function pre-conscious, that would sustain any psychic representation given, and, as we know, would be then the interpretation that would put the belief at issue, since this operation would be, perhaps, a previous step of the "dismantle" of the valid, accepted representations and exclusion.

However, on the other hand, if Herrmann enunciates that cannot affirm anything in addition to what the interpretation reveals, we can have the freedom of thinking also anything can deny and, as if cannot deny, it confirms the existence of the unconscious just as it is postulate by Freud, with all your qualities and characteristics presuppose.

We could, inclusive, go a little farther for that way to the think to see where arrived, since the only danger of the think is the misunderstanding, and it, whereby seems, is not lethal. Whether we face the postulation Freudian about the unconscious and consider that the theoretical statement is an interpretations set or a theoretical interpretation of the facets of the human psyche, of this possibilities infinite field, with Herrmann, again, say Freud's Statement about the unconscious.

Another Herrmann's affirmation that I propose to argue at this moment, and that, in the context that we saw in paragraphs above, it is right and logic of being, but that so much frightens the ones that with it come across for the first time and how sane as an amazing backbiting, it is the following: "There is no meaning in the sentence that affirms the direct communication between unconscious, neither can tell that an unconscious was captured, for posterior demonstration (Herrmann, 1991, p.335).

Well, such possibility could not really be enunciated by Herrmann, because, as we saw, the proposed psychoanalysis by he puts in this that would correspond to the systems pre-conscious-conscious and, being this way, would be a logic mistake affirm the existence of such a communication.

Want to do a comparative study between Herrmann's Ideas and the ones of Freud, but just using of points taken to be compared, seems that, for Freud, man of free spirit that was not refused to think and to speculate about the soul things, such possibility present was done and let that somewhat clear when it cared for a so polemic subject as it is the telepathy case, so dangerous subject at the moment, since we had one victimizes of the "telepathic jealousy", in case much more next to psychopathology than of the phenomenon in himself.

After saying being prone to believe in this kind of communication, Freud exemplifies, citing the insects behavior in their collective purposes and, like Darwinist good, speculates if the man, before acquire the communication forms just as we know today, could not have passed by an apprenticeship where another kind of communication would be dominant, for example, the telepathy, understood something above of the human nature, nothing of supernatural shadows or minds' divine properties, only a possibility abandoned during its evolution. Perhaps an example, extracted of the Freud comes to clarify how he faced the telepathy.

"She was in excess old of a numerous family and had grown with an extremely intense connection with her father. Had still young married and had found informs satisfaction in her marriage. Just a thing was missing in her happiness: It had remained without sons, could not, this way, put your beloved husband entirely in place of her father. When, after long years of disappointment, decided to submit her to a gynecological operation, her husband revealed that the blame was of him [...]. "After such revelation, was to Paris with her husband and, in the hotel, know of the presence of a fortune-teller. Dribbling certain reluctance by the husband, it managed to consult herself. "[...] she was 27 years old, but it seemed much younger, and it had pulled her married alliance. Monsieur Professor (the clairvoyant) reads told for she takes her land hand in an ashes tray inundation and studied attentively the mark let by hand; Then said you all things the kinds concerning about of arduous fights that waited her, and it finished with the comforter promise that, in spite of everything, she still would marry and to have two sons when it arrived to the age 2 year. When it told me this history, she was 32 years old, was seriously sick and without any perspective of some day has a son. This way, the prophecy had not accomplished; however, it talked about this without any kind of bitterness, with a satisfaction unmistakable expression, as if it was reminding a fortunate event".

We go to the interpretation formulated by Freud, just adding, that the numbers 2 and 32 had some significance for by patient, but that belonged to life context of her mother. "She (patient mother) there was married lately, not before having more than thirty years [...]. Their two first sons (being our patient in excess old) had been born with the shortest interval of possible times to each other, in one only period of a year: And I had, in fact, two sons, when arriving at the age of 32 lives. Thus, what *reads Monsieur Professeur* had told to my patient meant: Console herself with the fact of being so young? It will have the same destiny that her mother, that also had to wait long time by the sons, and it will have two sons when it has 32 years. Have the same destiny that her mother, put herself in place of your mother, take her place close to the father - outside this, however, the most intense wish of her youth, and precisely in view of the no-accomplishment of this wish is that she was starting to get sick" (Freud, 1996, pp.48-49).

The wish Oedipus complex of occupying mother's place and to have your father's sons was present and alive in the unconscious of this patient of Freud, who by the characteristic of being the unconscious no-time can thus keep waiting the accomplishment search. The fortune-teller, so, "captivated" a content of the unconscious (the incestuous wish) you know itself there why means. Such content (the incestuous wish) was unconscious for by patient of Freud, as well as for the fortune-teller, being, afterwards, unveiled by a third, that is, Freud itself.

But, where is the unconscious communication?

For patient communicated something of herself for the fortune-teller, without having any notion that it communicated, the fortune-teller communicates what before it had been her communication, as well, without the conscience that it was communicating, since the wish sullen there was if disguised with other it dresses before the being unveiled by Freud, your interpreter at that moment.

Unconscious for by patient and for the fortune-teller, but not for Freud. This way, have perhaps arrived well next to affirming the relativity of the unconscious, without discarding, however, that it (wish) can be relative.

It seems common thing of day by day, where the chance or for proximity does us observe a certain dynamics of a person, a tendency, for example, of find boyfriend and girlfriend boors and the involved person does not realize at all of her movement: Always hit in the target, even though are in the opposite that consciously wished. Certainly, unconscious for her and not to who observes, that is next to the referred person, rich in loving disagreements.

If we take the examples extracted of Freud and of our everyday, I think we will not manage to abandon the idea of a possible unconscious to of being captured, unveiled for "palpable", opening and not closing the exercise of interpret the beings who move your lives by the more strange and amazing motivations, with register, memory, thoughts and ready unconscious wishes to be captured.

It is not necessary no more profound comparative study to demarcate the how much Herrmann removes of Freud and, by the distance observation, have the impression that if treatment until of another thing, very different than many understand by Psychoanalysis. However, for more contradictory than that can seem, Herrmann we keep Freudian faithful to the Psychoanalysis, because so much for Freud as for Herrmann, the wish draws in the interpretation and, for being infinite dress them of the wish, many are the interpretative possibilities. The interpretation like essence of the methodological operation, the common and convergent point.

The divergences exist and are profound. Happily! Since the human mind continues covered by the mantle of the unknown. There you have the Psychoanalysis future.

2.5. A brief incursion in another field

It is not so infrequent to find the driven question to me by many colleagues, about the philosophic filiations of Fabio Herrmann, if his ideas do not find a foot in the "thought kitchen" of any philosopher.

Confessed my philosophic ignorance in first hand, however, do not manage to answer to such questioning is for pure lack of philosophical formation but, also do not let, is clear, of get curious.

And it was moved by the simple curiosity, that I solved venture me in this field, without at least have the pretense of accomplishing a philosophic reflection or of doing a tracking of concepts by Herrmann among philosophical schools, dissertation that would not have end.

I recognize first that Herrmann is much more Freudian than I perhaps like being; A hurried reading, it locate their ideas in the German idealism wake, passing, for example, by Kant, in the that burrow the real notion and, mostly, by Fichte, in the that burrow to the representation, thought Kantian main philosopher representative.

For Fichte, for example, the representation is going to be a conscience determination, a way to if it have conscience, it's on it itself.

If we think Freud enunciated that an impulse just would be well-known if it was connected to a representation and, otherwise, its anything could know, soon will give us to truss theoretical, of the likeness, at least of statement, from these three thinkers, Freud, Fichte and Herrmann. Finally, the representation like possibility and condition of being conscious and, for consequence, of being cognoscenti. The world, this way, just there is when it is represented and that that cannot thus it being, it will enjoy and it will remain fetter eternal universe of the unknown.

"I am subject-object and my true being consists in the inseparable identity of these two aspects". (Fichte, 1980, p.11)

The object, it appears here, like a fantasy separatist of the Me, that takes the subject to know in this division through the illusion of something exterior, that separates it of the world, of something, giving to notion of a provincialism and of a ghostly limit, that is, the notion of independent reality of being.

It seems, so, since I search similarities, that notion of a shield of two facsimiles one that would be identity representation and to other the one of reality, but that belong to a same shield, to the same individual, resembles to the Fichte's relation subject-object conception; The object like exteriorization, and the external part of the shield, heartfelt also illusorily like naturally external, since for the subject, having in mind the shield idea, the reality is going to be an external object and not the representation of this own subject.

Such likeness. Also gives, in my opinion, in that burrow the notion of Me, of the identity like surface representational engraving in the shield.

In Fichte (1980), the Me if manifest in the sphere practice horn a wish that needs a certain resistance to continue existing. Without such resistance, the Me cannot affirm your independence and if liberate. See itself limited, the tendency to overcome their own limits is going to if you do present.

The resistance announced by Fichte, it seemed to me, again, very next of the defensive idea of the shield where, through a part sequestrate of the real, the wish, CREATES in the internal part of the surface representational, of the Me, that for being detached of the real of which differentiated, it aspires by limits suppression, to melt itself again with the real of which stood out.

"All that that is here for we are produced by us ourselves. And this, no without a doubt, is an affirmation that contradicts frontally the common conscience. Not themes conscience of producing what it is here: We just have conscience that it is here" (Fichte, p.240).

Well, what we present like belonging the conception order, the unconscious, the real cannot have conscience, for being no represent able; Only can aspire to the logic of the conceived, of that, that could one way or another be represented and, thence yes, arrived the conscience.

For consequence, if drift thence our things reality firm conviction that are outside and inside our limits, since we do not take faculty conscience of its production and, already produced, if it presents us as concrete, absolute fact, that not if doubt.

For Herrmann, the psychoanalytical man is characterized by a crisis of constant identity, where the representations in both your surfaces, that is, the one of the identity and reality will go alternating itself and shocking itself, losing the characteristic exclude, a subject strolling through and by alternating representations. And, thence, by and through the representations has been to several worlds and loses, so to speak, the dread of if you see and have different realities.

The philosopher Fichtian it elevates above of the representation and is conscious of her, it has conscience that the objective world is a represented world and to for having such conscience, gets with freedom through the free reflection, that that the common man does with and from need, that is, grabs to the representations and of them becomes slave.

Finally, did not intend to accomplish any comparative study or to do a thought filiations genealogical rising of Herrmann who happen today in the Psychoanalysis; The goal was the one of just to accomplish a small incursion, imprecise and that has incompleteness mark of that that little or almost nothing has to philosopher, but, that by the simple curiosity tried to seize of its shadow.

The small incursion in this so complicated field as it is the philosophy, it was just tried with the purpose of accomplishing some notes, among them, to stress that Herrmann affiliates by thinkers that, practically, found the own psychoanalysis by the penetration value and of the thoughts weight that overtake the philosophical discipline itself and that infect a good part of the history of the think human.

Herrmann with its creative brilliant idea, it manufactures at present the past discoveries flavor, it projects in the Psychoanalysis like a national production of weight and that take force with by universality of your ideas. It puts us a Psychoanalysis representation that if shocks with the others, do not to be the victorious or denies them, but, just, a field in excess, opened so that the Psychoanalysis strolls by our eyes without dogmatism.

Chapter 3
The Interpretation in the Psychoanalysis

3. The Interpretation in the Psychoanalysis: The method essence

In your book "The Psychoanalysis Method", Herrmann revises a classical episode, the dream of the applied injection in Irma, dreamt by Freud and interpreted by him, to demonstrate for tautology existing in the interpretation Freudian, besides trying, somehow, a certain methodological depurations, putting in check the concept of unconscious formulated by Freud.

The proposed interpretation by Freud part, initially, of the dream consideration how it is reminded, that is, its content manifest. Afterwards, it divides the same into parts, could be, each part, starting point for multiple associations.

The objective final is the one of find an alternative text to the dream manifest, tell, its latent content; That is, thoughts full of significance that were deformed by the dream work so that the accomplishment of wish if of this of mould disguised in the dream manifest.

The operation that transforms the latent content in manifest is called by Freud of Dream Working (Elaboration), that, with some own characteristics, like the condensation, the displacement, figuration, dramatization, secondary elaboration, would defraud the censorship and would form the manifest dreams, enabling the wishes accomplishment that, for belonging of infantile nature, they show inappropriate to the conscious accomplishment, even though are in dream.

Herrmann it opposes to the formulation conceived by Freud, when it presents that the mechanisms attributed to the operation of the unconscious are going to make part of the method employee for the interpretation, that is, that such presuppose are going to be built-in in the interpretation, this way, the interpretation is going to find exactly what proposes to find, "because, simply, the processes attributed to the dream formation are the perfect reverse of those used to build its latent meaning. (...) That is, each one of the deduced mechanisms corresponds to one of the processes used to the interpretation: There be or not such mechanisms, after that translation process would proceed, since they are the ways back that the dream interpretation was the one of going."

Herrmann does us see how the same to presuppose used to if arrive to the interpretation do, on the other hand, the interpretation find your perfect reverse, as if the mechanisms (condensation, displacement etc.) went characteristics of unconscious and not of the method that already I had them how to presuppose. Finally, the interpretation created an unconscious reverse to presuppose that they a priori were your paradigm.

Well, like the good logic carries us to think, if that that we find in the "revelation" of the unconscious is exactly the reverse that we use as technical, like interpretation instrument, then the interpretation if exhibition as the instrument revelation and, there, for tautology.

What would be being revealed like content that lay unconscious, nothing more would belong than the instrument illumination applied, as if to the use a microscope applied in to analysis of a certain bacteria, it saw the properties of the instrument, its lens etc. and, to leave of this verification, that is, of the properties of the observed lens, believed that the bacteria has the appearance, the form of the used instrument.

And as result, would have, taking itself to the extreme absurd, prescribed antibiotics for the microscope and not to combat the bacteria. Displacement, condensation, figurative secondary elaboration would be, so, instrument properties applied and not characteristic of the discovery itself, properties of the unconscious.

With such considerations, we can tell that the unconscious Freudian does not pass of an interpreted contrary, that the attributed characteristics him nothing more belong than the reverse used in the interpretative process: On the other side of the condensation, the free association, that would form a countless text larger times than the dream text manifest; In opposition for figuration, the reversion in words, of the secondary elaboration, the reversion of the not critical to when associating etc.

Well, we know as Freud conceives the dreams. For him, due to the omnipresent censorship, however lowered by the sleep state, ideas, pregnant thoughts of wishes cannot be admitted to the conscience directly, being the dream manifest the result of a forces game, where conciliations and commitments are allowed so that, in peace, the subject continues dreaming, sleeping, since the dreams are the sleep guardians.

The wishes, in the dreams majority, are accomplished of disguised form, mostly when they would be expressing one wish repressed. And when such disguise is not enough to defraud the censorship to the repressed that tries its eternal return, the dream is accompanied of anguish and this, so, would occupy the place of the oneiric deformation, awaking the dreamy most of the time.

The dreams, for Freud, are conceived like a psychic activity that owns meaning, but, whereby notice, Freud faces this psychic activity in consonance with the postulation of a psychic device that works with determined characteristic and are such characteristics that would mark the interpretations Freudians. If it conceives the psychic device of another way, if we forge another representation of the same, could find this other way overlaps, embedded in the interpretation of a dream, of a symptom, of a considered act fail etc.

This way, Freudians interpret by Freud, lacayan, by Lacan, kleinian, by Klein and the interpretation, from this done, capture to a statute tautological, revealing the unconscious created for each one of the several theoretical perspectives, or of the formulations that presuppose an operation way for the human soul.

If really there are free forces that are dislocated, unconscious selective mechanisms of the psychic qualities in our mind, they would be own speculations for a psychoanalytical psychology, however, could not make integrant part of the psychoanalytical method, that, by excellence, does not overtake the limits just to of being interpretative.

"Only the interpretation applies for the Psychoanalysis, like knowledge methodological source specific. Being the unconscious only an interpreted, operational fault value to any affirmation about this one that does not start and finish in the interpretation."

As we notice, the unconscious stops having substance and concrete mechanisms of operation, just to be product, result of interpretation, nothing affirming or denying in addition to what it can reveal. The unconscious, in this exact meaning, does not exist, but there is. Prioritizing the methodological depuration, for each established field there will be a relative unconscious that will be led in the measure of its rupture. The interpretation, it liberates and purified of presupposing theoretical, will enable discover of so many possible unconscious as she herself allow, not saying and neither denying anything that be gone in addition to what it was interpreted, that is, that that the field rupture propitiated.

The unconscious stops concrete to be virtual of the multiple and heartfelt possible, significance that the psyche productions of an individual, of a collectivity, of a culture, will be able to come to reveal.

You seem that that denies here are not the theories, the speculations on the soul, the formulations metapsychology those needs to be well-known for the refinement of the think psychoanalytically. What we subtract are all the formulations embedded in the interpretation to liberate tautology fasts method, because, otherwise, will walk eternally in circles, discovering already well-known, yet thought and passing by top of so many life forms that are barred of the human repertoire for are not them enabled representations in the everyday life; We will walk in circles trying to catch the property "tail", because to each mental human formulation, the each construction of psychic device, these postulations, are built-in in the interpretation, will find what we embed, will discover the property "tail", although it are with strangeness and fright air.

However, the suspense still in the round and the doubt shadow still in discomforts. If is just that get, on one side, liberate us of the tautology of the interpretation, how can, so, know if it treatment a true interpretation, what really does it correspond to the patient's mental universe?

"Situating itself in the field transferer that, by definition, is the place of the potential effectiveness of the possible multiple, the analyst interprets, means , promotes the shock of possible representations with those valid, so that the loss of the limiting field lets come new possible and effective representations. If this other thing, the new representation, checks a coherent significant unit to the system representational, we say being in front of a good interpretation, in other words, of a true interpretation, that puts in new evidence field, unconscious relative new."

So that an interpretation can be considered true, two terms should be performed: The one of the productivity, that does come heartfelt multiple, and the one of the longitudinal value, that establishes relations more and more wide of the representations, allowing to glimpse the patient wish drawing, configuring felt pertinent and not disconnected each other.

However, once again the doubt shadow still in the menace! Would it be possible same to liberate the interpretation of all and any tautology? Question that returns and in the disturbs, not being convenient, at least to this height, hides it of the thoughts, since the interpretation Freudian certainty death let us orphan.

We know that the psychoanalysis method can be employed to any psyche production; If we think of field and rupture, in the interpretation like a new alternative representation to those dominant, can imagine if this new alternative representation does not run the risk of being subject interpreter simple product and that, for suggestion, do it proceed permeating individual's universe representational that was offered the interpreted being? If in part that occurs, will find, again, through the subject interpreted, for tautology of the present interpretation, sometimes since becomes impossible someone if transform in pure method. Or: The interpretations, by the characteristics of human subject, will have always something tautology, mostly when does not let our psychic device aside (and that is not any fiction) when we interpret, staying our presuppose individual embedded in the formulated interpretation, belong to a patient, in other words of a cultural production. Finally, if me turn free of the presuppose theoreticians still remain my permeate the interpretation.

Someone could give a just answer and not always so right. Sometimes, it is alone you pass some years in analysis to have the possibility to differentiate automatically what is your and what belongs to the another. I find it just like needs to pass so much time in analysis to differentiate what it is own and that not, but I think of field rupture process that is going to present an alternative representation that would be separated of the valid and dominant repertoire of a person, if in the construction of the same, the so much of interpreted would not be there represented and really is possible a pure exemption.

It went with these reflections and another similar that I came across me with a dream related by Herrmann, who does not reveal who it is the dreamer, only the dream and the interpretation, that I solved, do not know if to the right, do an interpretative exercise.

"A doctor has the following dream: It is in a rocky mountain, under strong temporal bone. It shelters with other people in a cave very large that contains, seems, all a city. In front, in the other extreme of the mountain, it opens identical cave, with people, houses, and highways. Sudden, it starts an avalanche and great stones are rolling, dangerously goes of a cave for another, for a long tunnel that interlinks them."

By the report know that the dreamer came suffering an ears inflammation, consequence of swimming and dives. The caves represented clearly the ears, the tunnel Eustáquio's Trumpets, the tempest would be the equivalent to the unpleasant noise, the cities in the caves would indicate the subjective size of the sore ears, finally, according to him, a body transposition to the mind. Finally and of blow, after other series of associations, the dreamer of the itself tells that he was to dream anything less than with the "temporal bone crag". Crag of the temporal bone in a crag. For Herrmann the dreamer would have a preference for representing metaphorically life state, a taste by the word and by the game of the same, with certain ironic intention, when playing with the inflamed ear and with the medical formation. A perhaps difficult patient, but not completely uninteresting of analyze.

Do not imagine of the dream author, but, difficult and not uninteresting patient attracted my attention. If Herrmann used a Freud's Dream to serve of speaker to his arguments, find, so, that also could use a related dream and analyzed by him.

As did not dispose, clear, of the dreamer's associations, divided the dream without any rigid system and proceeded associating in the place of that that dreamt. I transcribe now, a small summary of such associations:

"Under a strong temporal bone" - a tempest that puts in risk, in danger, who knows the to of being infected by the disease that tries to cure (the dreamer was a <u>doctor</u>).

"It shelters with other people in a cave very large that contains, seems, all a city" - cave very large, perhaps a certain dreamer's consideration for having accomplished a discovery and so much (I remind me that the children when they do camp like discovering caves) and how about discovery already had conquered a lot of followers, a whole city.

"Ahead, in the other extreme of the mountain, it opens an identical cave, with people, houses, and highways." - A next cave = a next city, that the dreamer intended to conquer. Would it be possible or not such conquest? So, present a preoccupation of win or of failure.

"Sudden, it starts an avalanche and great stones are Rolling, dangerously goes of a cave to another, for a long tunnel that interlinks them". - a courageous attitude besides avalanche goes of one to another. Avalanche...An avalanche of criticisms, the stones like disapproval.

Now, which representation if mould, draws, to be able to present as alternative to that configured by the dream manifest.

Perhaps a famous doctor that was in the prominence of pronouncing a lecture (or seemed thing) about your ideas, whose reception of the same was preoccupation reason, because could suffer an avalanche of criticisms. The dream then, it denoted an insecure person, worried, distressed by the pain of being scorned, putting thus for land, all conquest pretense, of profit, of gain, of recognition. He is an ambitious person, however insecure.

Freud teaches us that, after all, the dreams never have interest for things that we would not try worthy of our interest during the day, that the small things are discarded, are not worthy of our dream.

If we compare the gained interpretation the "middle ear" with the one that Herrmann presents us, we could even think the interpretation provided by Herrmann seems to be in a way of relief, of appeasement for the one that dreamt, because the fears and preoccupations that seemed to do great internal noise, did not pass of water in the ear, thing without much importance, that inconveniences, but not enough to deafen someone; As if the dream author had awaken of the dream by the own interpretation, that is, come in an other dream.

The dreams just are not wishes achievements, but they bring in your bulge preoccupations, fears and so many other things that make part of the mental life of a person. Like Freud, it agrees to do not refer to the dreams to a vigil life incoherent mental activity, in which the same own felt, however, not an only. And, for thus be, others interpretation possibilities could present itself, modifying all alternative hitherto built representation. If the exercise is attractive, I think it would not be any sin let itself seduce by the and to risk one more interpretative adventure.

We know that for Freud all civilized man retains infantile forms of his sexual life that, nevertheless, are substituted in the dream content for representation insinuations. Following this reasoning line, it could think the taken dream like example represents sexual ideas of an innocent way: The caves, the entrance and the exit dangerously, the subjective size of the ears etc., representing a sexual relation and, for being infantile, of incestuous mark. Who knows a medical married, worried about the discovery of its infidelity or one wish, accomplished or not, that drew the dream author like a conqueror of the little cave of its woman or of the neighbor woman?

In the dreams field the certainties are suspended. Perhaps not even the dreamer will be able to trust in the dreamt, mostly when it has in mind that between dreamt dream and the reminded, related dream, surplus another whole field for the dream "invented". However, cannot belittle, how the same determinations can be present in the psychic motivations of the dreamt dream and of the dream invention.

The interpretative options could be endless, I think other that come if it comes across with the dream example and the supplied interpretation, will have perhaps terms of supplying more and more interpretations. But, if such interpretations do not reveal the unconscious from who dreamt, - because of this same, our exercise is innocent and does not hurt the ethics and neither to anybody needs it offend - they bring for towing, on the other hand, presuppose them of the field established between book dream and interpret the "middle ear". Certainly there are contents of this interpreter in the field determination, but, the alone interpreter did not determine the field. I can tell that the related dream and the interpretation found in the book propitiated the formation of a new field, enabling thus, heartfelt multiple, "n" significances, opened field that are established between each interpreter of the related dream.

That is possible to escape of tautology do not am sure, because it would be impossible to turn exempted the interpreter of all his subjectivity. And, if it thus occurred, would be the interpreter finding his presupposes personal in the interpreted, since it would be the perhaps impossible did not embed them in the interpretation.

As we know, there is not pure perception subject or that is purified entirely by the method, as well as pure perception objects without variations and immanence from whom realizes it. If such arguments are worthy of credit, what is going to most weigh for the Psychoanalysis is that the analyst will not be free of his own mind and there, being until of little relevance as if it conceives the psychic device, especially when it interprets.

I understand that Herrmann's Formulations open possibilities to think of our theories, in our method, in the that we do. Especially when we believe in our creations, which transform the world things and that reflect your creator. Will it be that go out from the universe Kantian is a task still the accomplished being?

In the tolls to the methodological operation, the field idea, field rupture, meaning multiple possibilities revelation seem to give a status other to the psychoanalytical interpretation. However, it seems as well, that nevertheless, will find for "tautology" of the human psyche in all the felt that the interpretation can come to supply: The psyche and the psychoanalytical interpretation, the Psychoanalysis as the legitimate reverse from the productions encounter of the human subjectivity. The Psychoanalysis as a psyche science.

Chapter 4
Theoretical Applications

4. Theoretical applications

4.1. A Brief Evaluation of the Sexual Violence: Oedipus Revenge

We try to think the human baby, comprehend your intentions and pertaining to the soul faculties; However, only reach create an adult with which are habituated - that thinks, suffers, joy, simpler or more primitive. That is: To the try to think the baby, we think by him, retrorocket us.

(Fabio Herrmann)

In our actuality, especially after the Internet advent, are amazed, even terrified and alarmed with the infantile pornography transmitted freely, by the and among countless sites and electronic addresses.

The children are exposed in insinuating situations, some doing sex with some adult and, much more harrowing yet, another, nurse children, babies submitted to the varied tortures, whose instrument is for sexual compulsion, many times, present in someone of the family.

Little time ago, a Justice Promoter of Rio de Janeiro started to trace, and to investigate what it in fact passed with the children, especially when used in sexual practices, for signal, of the more sadistic and perverted. Changed, affected in its form more intimate reserve of the human soul, expressed its disgust before that the day it- day made public to the naked eyes.

Professors, dealers, men known as of well, enticed children, expose them publicly in photos and, even, nearby relatives, like parents and grandparents, they delighted in the sexual practice using itself of techniques, more similar to the ones of torture, than with the of the sexuality.

To have a problem dimension small idea, in the United States, at least one in four women was robbed sexually before arriving at the age of 18. Boys also were victims. A recent study showed that 30 to 46% of all the children were robbed sexually somehow before the 18 years (cited by Charam, 1990)

However, if we search a reason for these crimes, always, or almost always, find an explanation, who knows sociological, among analysis varieties schools, to turn the more intelligible irrational. The repugnance, however, overcomes the cold analyses, that do not convince the reason why of the human psyche to take so bizarre forms.

4.2. A first approach: The Symptom of the Social.

We could think, for example, that the inexistence of an agrarian politics, conjugated with the excessive ambition of the great economic groups that explore thousands of people, among them children and old, plays the human being in a miserably platform, in which irrationally culture and of the free impulses is a currency and of justified value, because, legally, the violence would banish what there is of human in the human, the respect by your fellow creature, the identity among equal.

We know, clear, that the people, when not more necessary, are devoured by the capital force and by the working lack finish emigrating for the cities and in them find adaptation enormous difficulties, becoming potentials for the rules degradation and of the laws, transforming itself in needy people of the more primordial resources that a person needs to exist, living in the great agglomerates of huts that are spread by the mounts and by the cities peripheries categories.

The poverty in which it lives the earth population immense majority could be a satisfactory explanation for any violence form, because it, itself, would be the incarnation that there is of destructive inside the human organism. People living in subhuman terms, that were not inserted and do not take part in the economic wealth, neither of that of the spirit, of the culture and of the civilization, now would charge its debt, exposing that they endure.

We find a reason for the violence apparently without rules, because of her; extract its logic and the cradle that welcomes them. But anything still would be enough!

For consequence, psychologists we beat with the modernity and the subjectivity construction in the historical process that is uncoiled in a nameless world. Men in good faith pray so that the world improves. Workers lose weight body and spirit in the working hours' dozens or of idleness brutalize, while its family degenerates in fertile environments in mice and insects. Blood streams for sky opened form and the tax to be paid is a ponder bit of life: The culture, the civilization conquests. Traffickers we multiply like heroes and benefactors of the needy communities. PM kills in an only day proportionally to a civil war. The widows cry. The sensible intellectual frightens. Many adopt pastors-German. Hunger children droughts and of love are tanned in cold blood in the middle of the See Square sun or of Candelária, with enamel or shoemaker's glue. There you have the fund of our portrait, of our perversity.

But the science conquests, of the technology and the cultural production that could raise the man for another platform of civilization, seem to have if lost like values, giving to impression that anything was created, developed, and that we come back to the jungle, now of stones, like re-edition worsened of our primitive ancestral.

4.3. Search Soul of the Violence.

When we stop to reflecting about the violence that took of our robbery society, cannot, besides the mud in which we will have to dive, stop trying understand a little more of kinds of the human spirit.

I think of unjustified, irrational, uncurbed violence. That perhaps just does not depend and only of the material terms, of the classes fight, of the cocaine traffic, of the mounts poverty, of the shoemaker's glue and neither of PM. Besides if do not justify by the wars that proliferate with the purpose of increasing the arms industry. That just like same violence the one that commits her manages to explain, and, sometimes, condemns and it martyrs, by you it practiced. Or it becomes distant and dissociated to do not feel blames when of the act memory that it was author. Finally, the violence generated in the being constitution bases, runs over it, plucks it of itself with the absolute power on the mind, having as a consequence acts that are projected on a defenseless victim.

Our pretense is the one of take Freud and the psychoanalytical school discovered a dimension of the human psychology that revolutionized our knowledge on being's psychic dynamic nature, putting to discovered the imaginary and the ghosts world that represent drives. The coin and its two facsimiles: Of a side, the father aggressor, trying to evaluate your psychic determinations and, of another, the children, passive victims and the countless sequels in your psyche, be in your relation with other adult, friends and in the internal resonances in your creative potential and of learning, in your insert in the culture and in the relation with life. Finally, the formation of its identity and of the aggressor identity in the bowels of an internal world blurred by the violence. Evaluate, identify, comprehend and to explain reflection exercises on the reality, where we lacerate the soul constitution.

As already we refer to previously, there are cases in which the general characteristics of personality of these parents aggressors, do not apparently do them differ of the normal considered men, without psychiatric antecedents, accomplishers of your duties, socially adapted.

Such intriguing circumstances carry us to make an attempt for rehearsal, of how and because, in an irrationality instant, these are taken to commit terrible atrocities against those, that, by the natural order of the things, should be protected.

It would be this uncurbed violence propitiated by the pulses, by the same form of pertaining to the soul operation found in all human beings, or, would it have occurred something different so that such dominant aberrant constitution was it done? Become the victims of this violence reproducers that it was suffered, an incurable wound in the device psychic

When we come across us with the news of the several communication means that relate cases of this kind, in which a violent father and beats ferociously your little son or defenseless little daughter, are revolted, disgusted, finish condemning the actors of such macabre histories. We immediately close the newspaper; we jump the pages and keep observing hands, to verify if the same did not stain of blood. Mostly now, when such subjects stopped exclusively to the brown told press and cross, practically, all the communication vehicles.

By the descriptions that are us many times presented and by the consequences of the atrocities of this size - when still remains us some reflection power, we can ponder with clean hands, that only a kind feeling of a revenge, it could justify such aberration. The victims, by its little age, become many times dissociated of the fact, when do not die by the consequences of the suffered violence.

However, cannot stop considering that "the psychological aspect of feel guilty is linked to the aspect relational of the participation and results from fact that the person who committed the abuse and the child is equally involved in the abuse in terms of interational." (Furniss, 1993, p.17) Is through the aspect international present in the sexual violence that can understand like the children, victims of such abuses, present, many times, intense feeling of blame.

For its side, the aberrant, when questioned, frequently answers that it does not know the reason why of the accomplished act, and if exhibition, not rare, also dissociated of the experience, nothing has to declare, reason some to justify.

However, frequently, like it points us Furniss (1993) take over completely the authorship of the sexual abuse like a psychological reality of the person can be a task incapacitated by the own structuration weakly of violently ego, in addition to what, there is a difference between sexual and physical abuse. In the physical abuse, the components ego concords additive generally is absent. On the other hand, the sexual abuse like an addition syndrome presents a dependent component, because the sexual excitation and its immediate relief can create the psychological dependence and the denial of this dependence.

At first sight, when we have in view the phenomenon, seems to us that only an intensified hatred could take someone to commit such atrocity, as we talk previously, something of the order of a true revenge irremovable, mostly when the victim is "deliciously" tortured, mistreated, burst, until the blood last drop disperses.

But, what revenge anybody could wish regarding a small child? What so brutal hatred would have a father against his small and innocent sons, that, neither they had time of enough life for so much it offends them?

4.4. The Psychoanalysis and the Soul Demons

Freud talks us about the feeling ambivalence, of drives duality, of drive of life and of drive of death. It reminds us of the situation oedipal which all the men pass like humanization condition, it teaches us about the seduction fantasies traps presented by patients that arrived at your doctor's office, besides to supply us an able to theoretical framework propose hypotheses and explanatory suggestions for such reason situations limits.

This way, initially think perhaps the phenomenon can be understood like an impulse incontinence of revenge, a revenge of something, that the today's author would have been victim in the past-present of her unconscious, re-editing and projecting for the reality something that only would have occurred to it in the fantasy.

We know that Freud, during a certain period was seduced. Seduced by the "seduction seductive hypothesis".

Such hypothesis convinced a scientist already of middle-age and with a baggage of considerable knowledge, to the point of such conviction if transform in a hysteria phenomena explanatory theory and of the obsessive neurosis.

In your article, of 1896, *New Observations On Neuro psychosis of Defense*, it postulated that "to cause the hysteria, is not enough occur in some subject life period an event related to its sexual life, that becomes pathogenic by the liberation and suppression of one affect afflictive. On the contrary, such traumas should occur in the tender childhood, before the puberty, and its content should consist in the real irritation of the genital (by similar processes to copulation) (...) Discovered that specific determinant of the hysteria - the sexual passivity during the period pre-sexual - in all hysteria cases (besides two masculine cases) that I analyzed" (Freud, 1896/1996, p.164)

It related thirteen cases, all of them serious and that should be considered like resultant of sexual offenses.

Further on, in this same article, says that "I myself would not give credit to these extraordinary discoveries if your complete reliability was not proved by the development of the subsequent neurosis. In all cases, several symptoms, habits and pathological phobias only can be explained retro ceding itself to these experiences in early life, and the structure logic of the neurotic manifestations turns impossible to reject these faithfully preserved memories that emerge of the infantile life. It is true that would be useless to try to extract of a hysterical these childhood traumas interrogating him outside the psychoanalysis; their vestiges are never present in the conscious memory, but just in the disease symptoms" (Freud, 1896/1996, P. 166).

While in the hysteria what we find while become ill factor is a sexual experience characterized by the passivity, in the obsessive neurosis, what we postulate is a sexual activity executed with pleasure that would return transformed in self-incriminations that emerge of the repression. However, the one that became obsessive, for having had in your childhood an active sexual activity, he would have been as well, previously, victim of a seduction whose passivity would be present. An effect in network. As if a kind thought "I was seduced, now am going to seduce" was put in movement. The sexuality would be, this way, awaken, invariably, for an older person. And the list of seductive was great, nobody escaped.

Knowing today of the ideas fallacy developed above and that at that time were defended by Freud, without forgiving the content but the form in which they present, can think in terms of the identity of that that suffers from sexual aggression, the effect in network could be framed like determinant of the future identity of the future also aggressor.

Freud betrayed by the wish that is in the constitution base of the human family, to the discovery edges of the infantile sexuality and still distant of decipher the enigma of the "Sphinx Oedipal", was momentarily devoured by Her.

Devoured, but not digested. It was wrapped up by the phenomenon; it took part in him as considerable part of your own personality.

Your auto-analysis, the Dreams Interpretation, it unveil of the pregnant fantasies of incestuous wishes of your patients and of himself, it enabled him submerge and to emerge of the profundities, releasing demons' soul fasts.

But, if Freud dropped into the fantasies oedipal traps and believed that the seduction really occurred and that that was the base etiologic of the neurosises, so, can imagine that such impression, like mark, should move the spirit. Inclusive the scientific.

If what was wished it can mark the psychic device like something that was accomplished and, seems also to us that the problem passed by that point, so, such mark, provoked by the wish can survive in the unconscious and, for some reason, for a defenses' in a way general failure, update itself as the compulsion transformed in act, since "the unconscious mental processes are of great frequency and meaning in the normal mental operation, as well as in the abnormal" (Brenner, 1969,p.2)

From the narcissism notion and trying to understand what if pass with family's human offspring, when they are born our babies, for example, that become, for signal, a parents narcissism projection and, if the narcissism it characterizes by the return, by the libido investment in the property I, could imagine that the ravished child would be the marks projection of the Me actualization, materialized. A re-edition in fact that it could have itself past just in fantasy.

Here, what observe is the weight of the psychic determinism, since in our psyche anything happen of spontaneous, by chance, fortuitous form, because, the psychic events are, go thus tell, determined by other that preceded them and with they maintain some relation in its current expression.

This way, from the result of game identification and of the consequences of the existence oedipal, by drive of death puts in action the device motor, expressing itself in an aggressive sexuality, re-editing a fantasy of frustrated love taking the form of an extreme violence act. There you have the revenge oedipal. Again the existence oedipal terms structuring and determining the backbone that sustains the human psychic operation; The tragedy that is gone constituting, weaving in the life of a person, generalizing itself in multiple facets, being the sexual violence, just one of them.

In your text of 1923, Freud establishes a Second theory of the psychic device: The one of the Ego, ID and Superego. Without intending to detail such theoretical aspects, that would overtake on very the limits now specified for the accomplishment of this article, Superego would be Oedipus complex heir, when the parents let of being investment libidinal objects and pass the identification by introjections being illustrations in the ego, like a precipitated, like a differentiated instance that is going to relate itself, inside of the psychic, with that same ego. With for introjections of the parental illustrations, they accompany as well, now as a psychic function interiorize, the demands and parental interdictions. "Although it is the renouncement to the wishes oedipal loving and hostile that is at the beginning of superego formation, this, according to Freud, is enriched by the ulterior contributions of the social and cultural demands (education, religion, morality)... the child's superego not if form to the parents' image, but, yes to the image of their superego; It fills of the same content, it becomes the tradition representative, of all the value judgments that subsist thus through generations" (Laplanche & Pontalis, 1983, pp. 645-646)

From this done, we can glimpse violent psychic operation historical constitution from superego images of your parents, that for some reason did not allow the social influences, of the culture, of the morality could modifies them, it enlarges them as psychic instance regularized. But which the foundation what would determine the so obscure and fateful bowels of a father violently? Would the mother have some importance?

We know that it is the mother who manages baby's cares. She is who gives bath, caresses, kisses, feeds, finally, excites body regions, denominated by the psychoanalysis as zones erogenous, that by your side, awake significances in the child mind, because "the fundamental is in the fact that the mother owns an unconscious, and that therefore the hygiene in general, the cares that dismissal to the baby are loaded of unconscious significances for her (...) The Zones erogenous not just because in them emerges a baby's corporeal tension, but above all because they are zones on the way physical and metaphoric, places through which ones externalizes and if interiorize a significance feelings carriers set. This precocious seduction maintains the essential aspects of the seduction in general, that is, the introduction of something in a still unprepared psyche for this experience" (Mezan, 1993, P. 33)

That seduction aspect generalized puts us in front of a great paradox: When the seduction is accomplished of violent form, what notice many times is the silence by the child and, on the other hand, when such human experience, in other words, when awake it of the sexual pleasure propitiated by the corporeal cares is significant afterwards, depending on the situation, what happens many times is the vainglory, the accusation that, for a process of characteristic operation of the unconscious, in other words, the displacement, substitute people of the parents become preferential targets. We can remember the case occurred in decade of Eighty in the United States and very well portrayed in the film *ACCUSATION*, of the director Oliver Stone, or in the city of São Paulo, at school of Base, in Aclimação's District, when the fantasy dribbled the reality and convinced thousands of people, especially after some children relate with details, have been seduced, used sexually by School owners and professors.

Some years later, they can realize how countless mistakes were committed in the investigation of the Base School case. However, the differentiation between reality and the fantasy is extremely delicate, because the psychic reality can impose itself to the facts reality.

Furniss (1993) tries such differentiation, not always it needs, doing a distinction between abuse like secret syndrome and unconscious communication. It points that "the child's sexual abuse like a secret syndrome can be many times maintained, accidentally, by the professionals who confuse unconscious and secret. The children in school age describe in compositions, the children in preschool age in drawings and the children in therapy through verbal allusions or not-verbal, direct or indirectly, your experience of sexual abuse... A child who writes, at school, concerning about of "a nightmare" and it describes explicit sexual matters; it can be punished for exhibiting a dirty fantasy... What seems to be unconscious material or "dirty fantasies" it can actually being a child's secret attempt of communicating the abuse reality" (p.47).

On the other hand, nothing guarantees that such "revelations" just would not be products of the infantile fantasy, of the psychic productions that, for signal, would be according to determined child's evolutionary phase.

We think, however, how more important than hastily consider such communications like true or not, it is the consideration by the child's psychic life, endowed of sexuality, worthy mental contents of respect and of attention, product of a ill and dirty psyche, or meaningless things of an infantile mind. The infantile being here an adjective of something little important or little developed.

For the child, of your side, becomes very difficult the help search, because, many times thinks anybody is going to give credit to her, that will be her the cause of the family discord, keeping its particular history solitarily for long years, until arrive to the puberty, when new terms enable the revelation. Only that then, your history, was already marked by abuse long periods and of sexual violence.

It is not infrequent that child's nearer family, especially the mother, proceed having doubt sentiments regarding the child and to the husband especially; But, by the sensations tangle and present feeling, nothing clear, confused, the doubts they waste in time, as something that should not have been thought and, this way, remote of the conscience and of the observation in the present time in which the sexual violence is perpetrated. This way, it stays the alone child, abandoned to your luck and to your psychic possibilities, with the formation of your pledged personality, especially when the parental illustrations, that they could be the pillars, its solid base of support, they are perversely introjected and, of inside, proceed dominating your psychic actions.

Conclusion

We notice, finally, that the related fantasies, in the Base School case, were convincing to the point of crush life of the involved, even when there was not any evidence, no acts verification that had supposedly been practiced.

Thus can conclude that the marks left in the unconscious, by the terms evaluated above, does not let any reality signal, so as to be almost impossible to differentiate in it what is true and what is imagination, fantasy reinvested of affection.

However, what does not fail to be intriguing in our evaluation is the fact that when it occurs for child's violation by an adult, especially when if it care for treatment own father, not rare, the adult alleges be pure fantasy of an infantile head, appropriating this way, like alibi, of a characteristic of fantasy, of the fantastic universe of the productions of the human psyche.

Chapter 5
From the Depression to the Suicide

5. From the depression to the suicide

Nowadays we observe, are in conversations with friends, through newspapers, of magazines and, especially, in our everyday professional, are many the considerations on the origins and the depression effects and of its relation, not always clear, with the suicide. "The Mr. Y is depressed and that makes him feels all life things of negative form". "You M improved his humor state and that made her resumed its activities". "H killed, because it was depressed".

The depression became to be a subject in the day list and is not few the ones that, actually, not even belonging to psychological or medical field, they improve in do diagnosis. It let of being a signals set and of specific symptoms, expression and result of a particular psychic condition, to they form generalizations that embrace life countless manifestations.

This way, the fact of a person just to meet sad or to express cry in a specific situation, can be the necessary and enough condition to be "diagnosed" as being in depression. Without intending to enter criteria about Humor Upsets diagnosis, it can think the depression involves including state of the psyche, enclose personality multiple aspects. It can, for example, indicate enthusiasm's state of a person, like the person evaluates and as it is evaluated by another. The problem, depression and its relation with the suicide, become, by its importance in all areas that work with the mental, modern and current health; Something that it cannot let aside, without a selected reflection of its multiple shade.

Solomon (2002) defines the depression like an imperfection in love, it marks that when it arrives, in a way general can degrade the Mine of the person and obliquity all its capacity at once giving or of receiving affection. People vary in facing of the depression, some are in fact courageous and another weak and can, inclusive, kill. However, if somehow all of them own a certain capacity to support some depression levels, also own the capacity to support it in many circumstances, be and continue it's in a way joyful and deigns life.

The depression is frequently related to decrease of the physical and mental welfare of a person, in the great majority of times, it reflects in its physical terms, in the appearance and in many behavioral evidences. If we take her like a representation, the depressive state can be considered like the relation unvoiced expression between mind and the body, what would mean a unit divided just under the semantic point of view. Recent studies (apud Solomon, 2002) point that from 2% to 4% of the depressed will be able to commit suicide for direct consequence or depression insinuation and that 50% of the population, in some life period, will be able to try some symptom related to depressive state. The depression comes victimizing people more and younger, reaching especially children in the varied of age bands.

Mendels (1972) says be the depression as old as the man, that accompanies it through the history and its description makes integrant part of the universal literature, because if it treatment a psychic so old condition and disseminated in the man, different from the common sadness for its intensity, duration and evident irrationality, as well as for your several effects in people's lives who of her suffer.

5.1. The several depression understanding searches

In the psychology, for (Dorsch; Häcker; Stapf, 2001), the depression is defined like a complex concept for lots of symptoms, such as bad mood, sadness, negative concept of himself, accusations and auto-reprehensions, schism, concentration loss, motive alteration expresses for agitation situation and/or of retard, interest loss, inability of taking decision, presence of insomnia or of hyper-sleep, appetite loss or increase and of the libido. With the Classification advent of Mental Upsets and of Behavior of Cid 10 (1993) and of the Manual Diagnosis and Statistician of Mental Upsets – DSM-IV™ (1995) it got some clinical-categorical unit for the depression diagnosis, however, with regard to its etiology, so much of the psychological point of view, how much somatic, the theories they multiply.

Just to situate the matter, Krech and Crutchifield (1976) care for the emotions linked to the depressive state, especially the produced by the success feeling, failure, blame and remorse. Such emotions would be essential determinate intimately linked to the perception that an individual has to his own behavior, or of your behavior regarding other standards. They say be evident that such emotions appear gradually in the child, in the elapse of your development, however, do not establish when the child would be ready for life them.

The success and the failure are conceived by internal standards of accomplishment and not by the exclusively social, external. These last, observe, exercise a great influence in the establishments of the internal standards and, in seen of this, people would arrive, until a certain point, to organize and to adjust your own standards in a significant relation with the ones of another. Like result of this relation, the individual would form a certain judgments conscience that to your respect are done.

The success feeling and of failure would be then propitiated by the sensation of whether it have reached or not a wished goal, and to leave of this condition, verify itself-went the pride profound emotions ebullition or of shame. The emotions linked to the blame, for its turn, would arise of the perception of a moral transgression, by the practice of determined acts. Such emotion, clear is, are relativistic by the individual existence, since the moral standards of accomplishment, in spite of being universalistic for the participants of a same culture, they enjoy of a margin of individual elasticity.

Allport (1966) thwarting some sights points of Krech and Crutchfield, it puts that a child two year, from the pulse frustration of characteristic exploration of this of age band, it can feel a shock in your self-esteem, result of an acute and conscious sense of herself, what denotes one I already very formed and propitious to develop depressive state.

In your research of how the I develop in the several of age bands the author points that, in the age from four to six or seven years, in our culture, the self-esteem acquires a competitive trace, staying this way, in the self-esteem development dependence, the presence or not of the humor upsets.

Giving continuity to your formulations on the self-esteem and of its relation with the depression and suicide, that personality psychology important theoretician adds that a lot of our social life is centralized in the self-esteem. For him, embarrass a man is to shake his self-esteem and the resentment would be an impulsive way of affirmation of the offended self-esteem. The pride and own love they constitute then synonymous for the self-esteem and for the depressive state.

For Jung (1982a), the I would be constituted by two just apparently several bases, a somatic and another psychic. The somatic would be well-known by somatic sensations that transposed the conscience threshold, while, part of this kind of stimulus; it would prosecute in an unconscious manner. The Ego would be supported in the global field of the conscience, subordinate to himself-same; in other words, the global personality cannot be captivated in its totality.

Still describes Jung (1982b) some psychological, resultant kinds of the adaptation combination of the functions: Sensation, feeling, thought, intuition and both basic actions of the psychic energy, for introversion and for extroversion. In the existence dependence of the inferior function, among others aspects, would be life of a predestined individual the successes being inundation or of depressive state, impediment of the personality potentialities accomplishment. The wide result of individuation process, it would be in a combination of the four functions that would enable an equilibrated conception and good of the world.

We also find in Reich (1975) the formulation that the character is constituted by the habitual attitudes of a person and of your consistent standard of answers for several situations, including your conscious values, behavior style, and physical attitudes, such like posture, appearance, body habits and movement. This author does reference to the genital character and to the neurotic character, being the first governed by the auto-adjustment principle, without the inhibitions of the moral principles, could abandon itself freely to the flow of the biological energy, unloading adequately the sexual excitation repressed by means of pleasing corporeal actions, in other words, a self-confident individual is world conscious and expert that surrounds it. To the neurotic character would fit the psychic solutions depressive.

Perls (1977, p. 79), then, points out that the person should be sight as one all, of way holistic, not existing in the human beings differences between physical activity, that that if pass in the body sphere, and the mental activity, because our bodies would be direct manifestations from whom we are. It conceives the man as part of nature, a biological event, as well as the society, postulates that each abstract notion is a process, as much as the visualization of an object. Deliberated activity, self-control, conscience, are social functions and at the same time, biological. The reintegration only can have success if all human activity, so much deliberated as spontaneous, thoughts and instincts is considered and treated like a biological process. Gestalt, so, would be the possibility than each organism owns to accomplish a great balance with himself and with its half and, when the terms for that are not present, would have the presence of factors that would take the people to suffer psychically and to develop depressive state.

There is margin to if think, through your presuppose general, particularly the illustration language notion and organisms fund, that the neurosis and the depression would be results of unfinished situations, where for gestalt would not have if completed. In case such language was listened, the person would proceed acting according to a reliable way of orientation, restoring the personality and building balance the way for a productive development, where the acceptance and rejection ideas would be linked to the orientation standard, to the need to of being accepted and to the fear of being rejected by the world.

In Skinner (cited Ferster, Culberstston & Perrot Boren, 1977) the body role would be exclusively in observable data and would have fundamental importance, because the people express behaviors, practice corporeal actions that reveal your feeling, your way to be.

Following this approach line, Lewinsohn, in the middle of 1900 (cited by Eber, Loosen & Nurcombe, 2002), marks that an inadequate positive reinforcement could take to an isolation and despair low self-esteem and increase indefinite cycle and constant and, as a consequence, to the depression

Beck (1967), based on your model of the cognitive triad (negative vision of yourself, of the world and of the future), notes that in the depression exists an interpretation mistaken of life happenings, involving negativism of self-conception, of the experience interpretation and of the future's perspective. More precisely, it presupposes a self-esteem lowered in practically all the felt, result of an erroneous interpretation of the happenings in which the person saw involved, determining this way, its future answer, in other words, a depressive form of interpret to yourself and to the world.

In the modern psychiatry (Ebert and cols. 2002) find the humor upsets, explained by multiple factors etiological. The biological hypotheses point, come in glandular factors, neurotransmitter, especially the norepinephrine, for serotonin and dopamine like responsible for such upsets, found frequently in the larger depressive upset, since antidepressant countless would act increasing neurotransmitter concentrations in the receivers' locations post-Sinapis, inhibiting its recapitulation by the rift sinapis. This way, through the action of the antidepressant the humor upsets could be influenced, controlled and cured.

Abraham (1970) was one of the first psychoanalysts to try to systematize the illness maniac-depressive, comparing the depression to the sadness or common suffering. It marks that the crucial difference between sadness, especially in the mourning and the depression is that the person by mourning suffers consciously by the entity lost, while the depressed patient is dominated by loss feeling, blame, low self-esteem and unconscious tendencies of hostility for with the person lost, be this real or imaginary, suggests that the depressive realizes the loss as a rejection and confuses her unconsciously with previous traumatic experiences.

Applying the neurosises investigation Freudian first results, Abraham (1970) argues that the neurotic anxiety originates of the sexual repression and that this origin differentiated her of the everyday, common fear that devastates people. In the same way, it distinguishes the sadness or sorrow feeling of the neurotic depression, being the motivated last and result of repression. This way, a neurotic will enter anxiety when your instinct suffer repression, preventing the obtainment of the waited satisfaction; The depression, for your side, would go to establish itself when the person is thank you to abandon her sexual goal to without having obtained satisfaction; Feeling not beloved and unable of love, it finds the despair regarding life and to the future. Such sufferings would last until its cause stop operating, be through real alteration of the satisfaction, or of possible psychological modifications of the ideas of unpleasant content. From this done, all neurotic state of depression, as well as the several anxiety state that accompany many times it contain a certain tendency to deny life.

For Freud (1996d) the denominated psychic instance ego is the part of the mental device that is in touch with the external reality and has as purpose guarantee the safety and the balance of the mental operation. The ego would be a part of the ID modified by the direct action of the outer world through the perceptive-conscious system. Therefore, it would be first, a corporeal ego, a mental projection of the corporeal surface, a kind of correlation intrinsic between our body and the representation that we have of in our mind.

Early the ego uses of stratagem to feel strong and valorized, seeking win the control about the ID. Putting itself as love object regarding the ID, like representative of previously directly invested objects, transforms a choice object erotic in libido narcissistic.

To glimpse as I was conceived the conception of the Me by Freud, necessary is done detain yourself a little in your positions.

In the *Ego and the ID* (1996d) he restructures the mental device, without abandoning your main concept, Oedipus complex. It specifies that the wider result of the sexual phase dominated by Oedipus complex can be the formation of a precipitated, consisting in two identifications species, united to each other. This ego modification confronts your other contents, like an ego or superego ideal. The ego or superego ideal, in this new conception of psychic device, would answer the all that would be expected of nature elevated most of the man.

With such theoretical formulations, Freud enriches the complicated woof in which wrapped up is seen as the I evaluates, staying this in the dependence of the internal relations among psychic instances. Some years before, in 1914, arising problems that would go to configure its new topic, in the third part of your article on the narcissism, Freud (1996a) refers to directly to the self-esteem, it considers it proportional to the ego size, in which a special psychic instance would have the function of providing that the satisfaction narcissistic of the ego ideal was insured, watching constantly the current ego and measuring it by that ideal. It argues the self-esteem so much in normal people as in neurotic and, especially the self-esteem relation of investments on objects. It marks that when the investment libidinal is corresponded, the person would have her reassured self-esteem, otherwise, your self-esteem would be lowered, because he would go to feel empty, devalued, for not having your corresponded love.

In the continuity of your considerations on the libido action, in *Mourning and Melancholy* Freud (1996c) search establish a relation between mourning and the melancholy, justifying itself for considering both psychological much seemed situations. The mourning is considered as a normal reaction to a conscious loss, dissuading, for signal, any intervention psychotherapeutic, once, when the person turns off of the investments in the entity lost, the process arrives to its terminus. In the melancholy can find, come in its main characteristics, a profound depression, the interest loss by life things, a drastic reduction in the capacity of love, the impoverishment of all physical activity and the self-esteem feeling lowering until to an intense auto-reproof point, auto-offense, arriving until to one wish delirious of punishment.

It pointed out Freud (1996c) that such self-esteem lowering is not found in the mourning, being, because, an exclusive condition of the melancholy. Such fact gives as a consequence of the libido action, previously linked to the object lost, but that, for a similar process, however more intense than repression, loses its mobility and, instead of to investing in other objects, it is transformed in identification with the object lost. What is observed, so, is just that the auto-offenses and other auto-attacks are in fact driven to the object that tumbles on the ego like a shadow. The suicide, so, following this thought line, actually do not would be killing, but, on the contrary, your target would be another object, another person that, for being interjected and identified in your own ego, he would have your destructive actions and of hatred, geared for himself. Such process can be described of the following form: Initially there was an object choice, in other words, a impulse fixation sexual to a certain person. By consequence of an annoyance, a fight or of a deception inflicted by the person sweetheart, the existing relation was destroyed. The expected result would be the object investment libidinal retreat at issue and its displacement for a new object, however, in the depression, such mobility is broken, occurring something very different. The libido it shows little resistant, it does not come back for a new object, becomes gathered in the ego, establishing an identification with the abandoned object. The outcome is the one of that a loss of an object it transforms in an ego loss and the conflict between ego and object beloved, it transforms in a split between ego and the person sweetheart, between ego criticism and the ego now modified by the identification.

For Fenichel (1981) the depressed patient complains about the fact of not being worth anything and acts as if it has lost your self, however, the occurred loss belonged to an object, so that ego and object are, under determined terms, compared. The sadism, this way, that in the past referred to the object, it comes back, now, against the ego, putting you next to superego and attacks the ego shown changed by introjections. Superego precedes with the ego in the same way that the patient, unconsciously, had wished to treat the object that was lost.

In the interaction dependence between ego and superego, Cassorla (1991)suggests the characterization of four kinds of suicide: Psychopathic, that is determined by superego interaction cruelty on the ego, obliging this to use psychopathic defenses; Maniac, where the ego see itself-went impotent and empty, like superego stimulating the self-destruction; Melancholic, in which the ego puts as aggression victim that is driven to the object, becoming thus alleviated; Schizophrenic, denoted by an ego in pieces, characterized by the confusion and indiscriminate, where the individual could attack and to kill an element confusing without at least to realize that such element makes part of its unit while to be. Concordant with Abraham's general opinions (1970), for Freud (1996c), the common point to all suicide the kinds would be the existence of a frustration libidinal, in which the wish could not be satisfied and, of magic way, the person would avenge obtaining as its result own death.

Besides the considered postulations, Freud (1996c) indicates that one of the particularities found in the melancholy is its tendency to transform itself in habit. In this process the ego recovers of the loss object and, for an investments accumulation in the object-I, becoming, so, liberate, what enables the regression to the state narcissistic. In other words, the habit would be linked to a sudden and disproportionate greatness of the ego that letting the critical instance aside, it becomes omnipotent, and everything gets easy and possible. It is as if the opened hands, they tried to grab the water; more precisely, it proceeds there being there some inflated egos that try to go besides its real possibilities, in a grandiloquent self-esteem.

It lifts the hypothesis that so much the melancholy regarding habit would be maybe in the terms physical chemistries dependence, still unknown, restricting itself to analyze only the cases that had been positively influenced by the psychoanalytical process that because of this, should have, like etiology, factors psychogenic, like the ones that we have just marked.

Such considerations on the depression dynamics lifted by Freud, can, in part, explain the suicide great occurrence in the population in general, especially among that suffer from serious depression, because, after all, the loving relations and your deceptions, with its countless outcomes make part of life of all the human beings.

Mendels (1972) considers that one of the causes of more important death is the suicide, this all over the world. More than 20.000 people commit suicide every year uses us, what transforms the suicide in an of the causes of commoner death. Taking itself in account that the data on the suicide and attempts hide more that they reveal, the true number of suicides probably can be 2 or 3 larger times than the data supplied by the official statistics.

Kaplan, Sadock and Grebb (1997) verify that the suicide risk between psychiatric patients belongs from 3 to 12 larger times than the not psychiatric, varying between sex, age, diagnosis, internment situation or external treatment. Psychiatric patients, in both sexes, have risks from 5 to 10 larger times of suicide than the population in general. Patient that never suffered any kind of internment, in both sexes, have the suicide risk from 3 to 4 larger times than the population in general. The population that commits suicide, in general, is constituted of middle-age individuals, while the psychiatric patients that commit the act are, in the majority, young. The victims' masculine average age belong to 29 years and half and of the feminine victims, of 38,5 years.

Countless are the factors that contribute for the suicides increase and attempts, thus with the schizophrenia, drugs alcoholism dependence, personality upset, that of implicit or explicit form, they relate with the depression, which seems to exercise a central paper in the problem. The feeling of blame and despair that attack the depressive can take it to believe that deserves in fact to die, or, so, that is preferable to die that live as it lives. It is considerably difficult to establish the relation needs between depression and suicide, however, in a study involving 134 suicides (apud Mendels, 1972) was verified that 94% these people had state under psychiatric treatment before the act suicide and that 45% met depressed.

The patients depressed rarely commit suicide when they are in the acuter phase of the disease. In this apprenticeship can observe a retard psychomotor profound that prevents the necessary action for a suicide attempt. The larger risk period occurs in the initial phase of the disease or when gives to symptoms remission, with the depression intensity decrease, when the person seems to have a certain recovery narcissistic and have enough energy to try something against her.

Contradicting Freud, Abraham, Fenichel and good part of the psychoanalytical literature, Bibring (1953) says that the depression is a primary affective state not-related with the geared aggression into, being the aggression, in a number of cases, the ego conscience of your abandonment, presenting itself as a secondary and not characteristic phenomenon of the depression, describing it like an ego self-esteem partial or complete collapse, mostly when this feels unable of reach your aspirations, your ego ideal, when these aspirations kept of intense and unshaken form.

Taking some Freud's Formulations, mostly in the that tolls to the aspects identification of the ego with the object, Jacobson (1971) comments that the melancholic patients they behave as if they in fact went the investment objects lost, although not taking over the characteristics of object. With that, the ego proceeds being meaning like a bad object, becoming a superego victim.

With regard to the relation among depressive state and the suicide, Gabbard (1998) says is the suicide associated of more contusing way to the larger affective upsets, not discarding the biological or psychological determinants, postulating that all the modalities of available somatic treatment should be used intensely accompanied of an approach psychotherapeutic. It says that to if evaluate the suicide risk, the aspects psychodynamic should be inserted and considered to a set of other risk forecast factors of short and of long term, such like panic attack, psychic anxiety, pleasure loss or important interest, depressive disturbance involving an anxiety humor drastic change for the depression, alcohol abuse, decreased concentration and generalized insomnia, despair, ideation suicide, intention suicide and historical of previous attempts.

Using Rorschach's Test, Smith and Eyman (1988) try to identify some relations object operation by ego and forms standards internal that could differentiate the people who make true attempts" of suicides, these just accomplished "suicidal gestures in the attempt to call people's significant attention of his a little family, affective. The of the first category presented an inability of abandoning first childhood wishes of receiving cares, accompanied of the conflict of being indeed dependent; A profound and ambivalent vision about the death; Excessive control of the aggression; Intense idealizations.

For suicide's psychodynamic seems to be profoundly rooted from the beginning of the constitution of your personality, preferentially established in the way like the Mine constitutes from your relations object primary, that would enable, future a situation of unconscious conflict that would determine the oscillation humor and the outcome suicide. There is a theoretical confluence with Abraham's Ideas (1970), Freud (1996c), Fenichel (1981) with regard to the present unconscious determinations in the suicide, the one of that this would not give by chance and neither it would be determined by some specific moments, that in a despair act, pure and simply, would make the person put an end to her own life. But they would be entailed to the losses objects, the loss of something (a person, a cause, the idealization of himself etc) that is heartfelt profoundly and that the ego does not manage to repair.

5.2. Depression in Childhood

The majority of patients who are attacked of Larger Depressive Episode present like characteristic trace a depressive humor or the interest or pleasure loss, predominant for at least two weeks and provoking an intense suffering and limitations in the social, occupational, affective operation. However, in many children and teenagers do not find the presence of a sad aspect, but, on the other hand, they show irritable and irritating and feeble same. The Depression in early life and same the suicide seem to own any peculiarities and to understand like by children psychodynamic if prosecutes, can, somehow, also throw some light on the depression development in people in general.

Melanie Klein (1982) structured good part of your theoretical conceptions from Freud's Formulations (1996d) about drives duality, established, in general lines, starting from your rehearsal *Besides the Pleasure Principle*, written in 1920, and in the mind's structural aspects, the ego, the ID and superego, developed in 1923.

Modifying and enlarging some of the original conceptions of Freud, Klein (1982) postulates that from the birth the ego owns feeling terms the anguish and of using defense's mechanisms, besides having terms to establish relations objects in the fantasy. The incipient ego, this way, in Klein's Vision (1982) deflate, in some measure, part of the impulse of death for the exterior and, starting from such projection, originates the fantasy of a bad object, persecutor that would threaten of destruction the ego. Such primitive ego suffers, from this done, the death impulse action and projects it like defense against the fear of annihilation. The impulse of life, for its side, also is projected with the goal of creating an ideal, good object. Such projections give on the original external object, in other words, the maternal breast, what a starting from then, becomes divided, organizing child's experience that it would be good and that it would be bad.

This initial psychic constellation, Klein (1982) denominated of position esquizo-paranoid that lasts of the birth to the 3rd or 4th existence month, for being characterized by the anguish of being broken by the objects persecutors and by the fact that the ego is divided. The central conflict in the position esquizo-paranoid would be a duality expression among impulses of life and of death.

In the measure in which the child goes developing herself and the ego having more resources, the mother can be felt, seen like a total object, could the baby loves it like a whole, not fragmented person. For this in a way whole mother sweetheart is that the baby it comes back to tranquilize his fears persecutor, seeking interjected it so that it get protection of the internal and external persecutions. If taken the whole mother like love object and of identification, its absence, heartfelt like loss, is intensely life, giving origin to a new set of feeling and reactions. This new form of the psychic operation, Klein denominates of depressive position, where it occurs the ego integrant and of the object, becoming the conscious baby of his own pulses and that the objects own an independent life.

For Klein (1982), the fixation point of the psychic diseases would be in the position esquizo-paranoid and at the beginning of the depressive position, where would recede the larger children, teenagers and adults attacked by the depression. However, they are the loss repeated experiences and of recovery by the which ones passes the baby, that turns your enriched ego, giving him confidence for the establishment of a safe object, that I protect it and enable support the depressive anguish, without carrying the person to the disease; This way, inside this particular vision, the existence and the adequate elaboration so much of the position esquizo-paranoid, as of the depressive, would be forms of if prevent the psychic diseases and of enabling to the individuals, future, face the losses, reverting of life.

Referring to the danger of the concept of depressive position to become some permanent explanatory references, fixed, worthless etiologic, Marcelli (1998) marks that the depressive episode frequently occurs, starting from a happening with loss value or in mourning, like parents' separation, the death of some family, the residence change, the death of a pet, the loss of a toy. These circumstances child's behavior changes visibly.

For Spitz (1993), the environment exercises a fundamental role in the child ego organization, passing by the stages pre-object and object relationship, in which the stay of a stable object and of confidences, as well as its opposite, the absence, the inconstancy are determinate factors for the ego development variations of the child. The effects of this variable object-environmental can be observed in the child activity general lowering and in the somatic manifestations by which are the children pass, when they are remote or lose parental illustrations whose previously established links are broken.

The indicative signals of depressive episode should be altogether, with time of duration and with child's behavioral changes. Among signals indicators of depressive episode, always carrying itself in count child's age, can consider the drastic alteration in the school performance, shiftiness in the appearance, apathy, absence of affective reactions, frequent accidents in which the child in fact hurts, aggressive, low conduct tolerance to the frustration, sleep difficulties, nightmares, sleepiness, appetite disturbances, enuresis.

Many of the signals and symptoms that the child presents can pass unnoticed even by the parents, could be interpreted like obstinacies, rude several or acquired idiosyncrasies. All this is indicative of how the depression in early life is difficult to of being recognized, not by clinics but, and especially by the family.

Aberastury (1984) warns that when the adults have difficulty talking with the child on the death, especially when there is the loss of somebody dear for the family and also for the child, doing circumlocutions or inventing story, there are as a consequence an impediment in the mourning elaboration by the child, impelling it to wish to follow the way to the person lost. The child has death perception and reacts according to the terms and resources propitiated by its infantile ego; Since the birth she faces losses, it suffers with them and when impeded from knowing the destination of your dear entities, for difficulties that the adults own when facing the losses, it can develop failures in your development ego, solving or denying the pain of magic form, that will future be able to transform itself in a psychic weakness, turning it unprepared, vulnerable for future situations, predisposing it at depressive state, for not having a sufficiently strong ego to work with the mourning and with the absence.

Marcelli (1998) points that some aspects appear regularly in the child's family environment who suffers from depression. Come in these aspects can detach the history of family depression, especially of the mother or of the father, that enables with which the child, still in formation phase and avid by identifications, becomes similar psychically to progenitor depressed, or it acquires a feeling generalized that the mother is inaccessible, the feeling that the child does not own qualities that attract interests it of the mother and can with that satisfies it; When one of the parents manifestation rejects the child, or the presence of an accentuated educational rigidity, enabling the constitution of a superego severe and punitive, including the children victims of sexual abuse, because we sit down responsible, blamed by the suffered abuse, condition this responsible for the child's victimized silence.

5.3. Depression in the adolescence

When we board the thematic of the depression and suicide, cannot stop focusing a particular phase of the human development, in other words, the adolescence. It is in the adolescence phase that occur typical inquietudes, as it understands the psychoanalytical theory, an evolutionary phase during which the person establishes her adult identity, an important moment that encloses all a maturity process. This way, in the adolescence is that is going to occur the definitive dismissal of the objects of infantile love and, for that, the wishes oedipal and its concomitant conflicts come back to arise. That interior breaking with the past shakes teenager's emotional life until his core, opening new horizons, doing arise hope, but also, anguish and fear.

Boarding the thematic of the suicide among young people, Freud (1996b) in your brief article *Contributions to a discussion on the suicide*(1910) points do not be correct to also affirm that by the suicide fact occur among young people not-students of high schools, would not exempt these of the responsibility of precipitating some causes, because the high schools finish replacing the traumas that the teenagers would have in other places and, that for your side, should supply to their students support and assistance in a life phase in which the peculiarities of your development propitiate a certain loosening in their family liaisons. And, in this aspect, stop accomplishing with its function of supplying the young people with family's substitutes and of in they awake interest by life and by the extra-family world. School read with immature people, and cannot bereave the right young people to remain in any apprenticeships of your development, even though such apprenticeships can be unpleasant

That parents' dismissal as love object, in other words, object investments retreat takes to an overvalue of the Me, to an self-perception increase by dint of the proof of reality, to the an extreme sensibility and auto-absorption and, generally to the centralization in himself and to the auto-enlargement, that that we call overvalue narcissistic, that takes the teenager to see his parents of another perspective, now not more so valorized as in the first childhood (Blos, 1985). The teenager suffers a real loss in the renouncement to his parents oedipal, and it tries an empty inside, suffering, sadness, that are parts of your mourning. The work in mourning by the childhood parents, by the infantile body and by the infantile identity, is one of the more important psychological tasks in this period, because the process solution in mourning is essential for the objects liberation lost, since Oedipus complex decline is a slow process and that arrives until the phase teenager end.

As well as we know from the psychoanalytical literature (Blos, 1985), is in the adolescence that the ego ideal comes to be constitute, like a superego, resultant of the Oedipus complex wide outcome, a formation intrapsychic, relatively autonomous, that serves of reference to the ego to appreciate its effective achievements, a special psychic instance of censure and of auto-observation. And, in case such the ideals become extremely rigid and demanding, the tasks to what proposes the teenager, by the occurrence of a simple happening, can take to a failure feeling of wide spectrum.

Superego is not a simple rest of the primitive objects choices; he also represents a reactive formation against these choices. This relation establishes the precepts that the person should be this way, but, as well, orders what the person could not be. It seems to us that, when superego demands the perfection, makes the teenager feels distant of reach your objective and becomes, according to your internal references, a heartfelt person as disappointing.

In the burrow to superego, we know how the same arises of identification with the parents, or with parents' superego, taken like model. All identification of this kind has nature of a desexualization or even of sublimation and, when that occurs, is in front of a separate drives. Such separate implies in the love separation and of the aggressiveness, doing this way, that superego increases its severity, because, by means of the identification and sublimation work, the ego contributes so that for impulse of death of the ID obtain control on the libido, making superego sadistic and destructive. For the ego, therefore, live it means the even though to be beloved by superego (Freud, 1996d). The teenager when in its personality constitution owns a superego punitive, sadist, maybe derived of its fantasies and of the progenitors demands assimilation apparently perfectionists, an efficient mother and of the representation of a strong paternal illustration, flawless and few accustomed to the reflection, they affect decisively the affective and effective world of the teenager.

The family nucleus, for its multiple implications, and by the fact that, in our culture, the teenager remains a considerable time in his parents' dependence, should be accompanied of an adequate evaluation, once to the crises teenagers corresponds the wide crisis of the family group, because, not rarely, the parents revive, for your side, in the adolescence of your children, some important traces of your own adolescences. Your reactions to the crisis teenager of his children are determined by the form as it solved their processes teenagers, what puts in check the family capacity of redefinitions and of new adaptations that the adolescence of your children comes to put.

Mackinnon and Michels (1992) say, in general lines, that all people own people's internal mental representations of her life, inclusive of herself. The personal representation, like object representation, can be very needs or grossly distorted. It uses the term self-confidence to describe an aspect of this auto-representation, that is, the image that the person does of her accomplishment own capacity. Beyond of this self-representation, or mental image of how is each person has an image that it would like to be or of that that thinks should be, in other words your ego ideal. The degree as this auto-image corresponds to the ego told ideal constitutes the measure of its self-esteem; inversely, in case it feels far away reaching your objective and aspirations, your love-own will be decreased.

We can understand that, when the teenager seems to do not correspond to his ego ideal, considering itself a failed, the result is the one of a shock in its self-esteem. The shock in the self-esteem and the self-confidence consequent reduction, they are primordial symptoms found in the depressive state.

Love-own of the largest part of people with tendency to the depression it bases in love continuous absorption, respect and approval of the important illustrations of its lives. These illustrations could have belonged to person's past, there is much introjected, or to correspond the external real illustrations, of present importance. In any of the cases, the rupture of a relation with told people represents threat to love and gratuity source, that supplies feeling narcissists.

We also can consider that the motivation for the apparently irrational act of take life can be considered itself as a dramatic attempt of communication. Such suicidal gestures, when the communication purpose does not obtain success tend, as there is already it very knows in the psychiatry, to repeat itself, many times taking the subject, in fact, to the death.

For Levisky (1998), for psychopathology can install itself when the teenager if fixed in narcissism solutions, taking refuges itself in the isolation and in the fantasy, in which the omnipotence and the idealization, many times of the destruction, occupy the role. Nowadays that teenagers' psychopathological perturbations is observed, far from disappear spontaneously, progress, giving continuity in the adult's pathology, especially when does not occur an appropriated intervention. Such psychopathological manifestations of the adolescence, certainly, threaten with the deviation or with a definitive stop of the development, especially when express in suicide attempts.

Chabrol (1990) clarifies, that the suicide attempts in the adolescence link to the depressions and that these manifest for a reduced and atypical semeiotics, like feeling of lasting and unbearable tedium, oscillating with intense nervousness periods; Dependence or isolation exaggerated regarding parents and friends; Sexual promiscuity; It tires; Corporeal preoccupations or physical symptoms; Appetite perturbations, of the sleep or psychosomatic disorders; School difficulties; Anxiety symptoms, obsession, phobias; Asocial or delinquent conducts.

The depressive humor in the adolescence is intimately related to intimacy lack with the parents, as well as to the social isolation. The normal adolescence has been considered as a separation-individuation phase whose difficulties are harnessed to the separation existence, because, the autonomy search can expose the teenager to a loneliness intolerable feeling and of abandonment culminating with the annihilation menace and, on the other hand, the dependence search represents a coalition symbiotic with the mother and for re-incorporate destructive. This way, the teenager is daily confronted with an impasse in his development that can express for a depressive semeiotics.

The depression psychodynamic comprehension in the teenager implies in the analysis of the family operation past and of its operation at present, which, largely, accomplishes a certain actualization. The teenager's difficulties can, this way, remit to the parents originated development conflicts afloat with vicissitudes of the son development. The depressive problem of this has been being related with the conflicts not solved of the childhood and parents' adolescence that can then it worsens it. The hostilities relations and the rejection attitudes that they condition in the family occupy an essential place in the depression teenager genesis.

As we saw previously, reactivations of the conflicts teenager's oedipal and those of your parents are in releases interaction. The parents' wishes oedipal or the defenses that create against they influence your youth's attitudes towards the body and to the sexuality of this. The anguish and blames it oedipal projected on the son or the seduction attitudes or of envy, equally culpability for him, pledges the sexual body integration that they do try as bad. The parents revive, through the son, the difficulties itself. The sexual body of this it identifies with the body of its old adolescence. The difficulties that had to accept your own sexual dobby can do it refuse the sexually mature body of your son.

At teenager's individuation can be disturbed by the parents' projections. For reactivation of the conflicts oedipal and of the dependence conflicts of these can take them to project in the teenager the bad parts and rejected of themselves and for externalization in your relation with his teenager objects internalization pathology. The teenager should alleviate the parents of that that they reject in themselves. It becomes, so, the trustee of the bad parts of the progenitors with which ones identifies in the measure in which they remit to your own conflicts and to its objects internalize relations pathology.

In response to such development conflicts found in the adolescence, the depression can owe itself for multiple mechanisms, many times intricate. It can be, this way, gratifying a reaction to the loss of the imaginative union with the mother, to the frustration of the libidinous needs and narcissi, to the aggressiveness against the parents internalized or to the aggressiveness return against your own Mine and your body; It can be a protection against the submission to an almighty mother intruder or, on the other side, the acceptance and the update of the teenager emotional life refusal by his parents.

Whereby if note, the depression can change negatively the social development. The depressed teenagers tend to isolate yourself or the rejected being by your friends. Doubting of your own value, they think they cannot be accepted except for imitation of the, what turns them vulnerable to the negative suggestions of the group to the drug use, of the alcohol and to the participation in sexual activities. The isolation and the social passivity jeopardize the behaviors learning opportunity of the communication that are become deficient.

The depression multiple determinisms they express in the meanings and in its truly contradictory functions. The depression can propitiate some ambiguous, ambivalent communications. The depressive behaviors can have value of a not-verbal substitute communication of the verbal communication of which it reveals the impossibility or refuses her. The depression represents a hostile message of reproof but it is, equally, a aid request, one scream hopeless of love and comprehension.

Whereby yet saw, does not belong to if it find strange that the suicide be one of the death main causes in the adolescence, since the biggest attempts rate appears on this phase. Suicidal behaviors of the teenager answer at multiple determinisms whose interactions with the depression not always they are clear. We know, despite all existing complexities, that the depression is responsible for suicidal behaviors, they own a causality common, come back aggression against the subject, however, at the same time, for more strange than can seem, the suicidal behaviors can represent a defense against the depression or, on the other side, the depression can appear as a defense against the suicide.

These considerations take us to deduct that the suicidal conducts can seem a way of avoiding confront it with the depressive suffering. They present a control and triumph aspect of the Mine on the dependence to the object. Exposing itself to the death, the teenager it affirms as the owner of himself. It denies its impotence and your abandonment and reaches an omnipotence illusion.

Finally, a teenager who tries to commit suicide, somehow, in other words, unconsciously believes that it killed a part of himself: Try to kill can mean that, imaginarily, a part of himself was killed and that and person keeps, somehow, relation with her. Thus, fastening this part dead of you in the psychic operation, the suicide attempt comes to give continuity to the depressive state.

With these considerations, we can with much clearness consider that if a teenager tries suicide, your development process is pledged and needs help, not only with measures and conducts medically, but also by a process psychotherapeutic that can involves him, as well as the ones that surround it.

Herrmann (2001) does not board specifically the depression and the suicide but contextualizing a psychoanalytical and social analysis of its determinations, having like instruments the Fields Theory, search running through the ways of how the Brazilian owns an auto-representation, while people, that it could be qualified of low esteem that would propitiate feeling and fertile relations for the depression establishment.

To understand a little this investigation accomplished by Herrmann, it would be interesting enter and to detain us in your representation concept.

The representations at the same time in which they make part constitute the man while to be cultural. Imagine a surface with two sides, a concave, returned into, representing the identity and another, convex, returned outside, representing, then, the reality. They own origin and purpose and is kept by a psychic function pre-conscious, denominated Belief, that makes the representations as concrete as the men that build them and defend them. Both the surfaces would be in constant new formation, and they would be built with defensive ends, some special apparatuses that detaches the man and differentiates it from the real, of the infection kingdom, that is, of the state in which the limits Mine-other, subject-object they melt and the whole reference system of a person or of a collectivity in an indifference extreme is lost.

The wish would be thus the sequestered part and differentiated from the real that, for having been detached and separated of the same, tries return him and it directs to him, drawing the subject, covering it of multiple dress, giving it identity, producing meaning. The failures, therefore, in this surface representational formation process, they could propitiate to the subject confusion state, losing its main function, the one of things kingdom defense.

When the defensive function of the representations, that is, when the belief becomes shaky, it escapes the reality meaning that before the subject owned. The identity, for its side, also gets trembled, and its individuality correspondent notion is posts in check, threatened. The subject realizes indifferently risk, of the dive in the human stratum of where emerged, that state cans today call madness.

Herrmann (2001) affirms that the belief fragility denominating it of faith, an extra effort that is demanded by the individual to try to keep his representations, so much the identity regarding reality. They are, so, the representational surfaces that guarantee the person to live within a certain logic, of some parameters to if guide in the life, even when the representations restrict to the theoretical lines of the psychology or to the political tendencies and to others so many constituent ramifications of the human universe: Whole nations, creeds, races.

We are not different from other human beings. Perhaps be, although less and less, somewhat how distinct in our surface representational. It is the set of our representations, that underwrites the wish of a people, what characterizes its reality, that seems shaky in its function especially starting from outside, with interpretations that we are not, that propitiate us abandonment feeling, of feeling that could frame itself in the low esteem category, culture broth so that psychic factors determine social terms in which the depressive state would be fertile.

The psychological theories diverge to each other, certainly, but do not fail to have an abstraction quality, of hypothesis than if raisin with the psyche. The psychologists need not to feel uncomfortable with neuroscience discoveries, because the mechanisms that move the diseases have origin in the human soul, that we do not let reduce the physiologic interactions or simply determine by the combinations of proteins.

We are in another field that is not possible reduced being. The psychology object, does not matter which the theoretical preference, it situates in a cutting of the different real from of other sciences. Our epistemology is product of a relation with objects that if list by methods, by very particular ways of investigation.

For our patients does not dissuade the means search adequate of prevention and treatment that can assist in your self-evaluation, mostly when there are worrying and propitious indicators for the development of depressive state. The psychotherapies, for example, perhaps be the touch stone, an important step to feel admired and esteemed by people who are to around it, contributing to modify the form as if they conceive, as if they relate with the properties that are them immanent.

After all, the sensation of joyful feeling of we ourselves cannot be something delegated to a second plan, or to an illusion just of surface, since we only have an unique life and lives it well and in its fullness is what it remains us.

We are taken to deduce that the object relations development good, affective, of reception and of support adequate in early life, they can propitiate the establishment of a safe ego, with feeling of adequate self-esteem and of proportional exigencies to that is you possible. It is necessary to stress that the environment in yourself is not a determinant only for the mental health, however, it completes it with existence of internal experiences and that assist the person to the development of the positively personality to face vicissitudes that life provides. If, for example, have a dissatisfaction with the form of our body, or with our habits, will be, without having conscience of our actions, influencing other with our attitude, favoring thus the creation of vicious circle, in which the if do not like it generalizes in rejection feeling. In other words, our ego, and for our consequence self-esteem is lowered, we will look the world and people of negative form, and thus will think we are being looked, a projection psychic mechanism clear example. That fact carries us to consider that even if caring for a depression determined by a neurotransmitters unbalance, the mechanism that move the sentiments, the actions meanings and of the general psychic action, they are strictly psychological.

It can consider, therefore, that the depression is related to lots of factors: Psychological, biological and social. The fact of do not have a positive evaluation of we ourselves, of do not like us takes and it is result of internal psychic state, profoundly rooted that are spread by the world in comes back. The providences outlet to improve the ego development, searching a landing in which this is in syntony, nearest in the ego ideals, can influence of positive way in the world conception that owns a person, in its auto-evaluation, in an adequate and necessary self-esteem for the reality vicissitudes facing. The narcissism not always it is pathological, especially when the body, possibility for all illnesses, needs an attitude that can reflect, even through the pain, life drive force.

The depression, a subject that much talks in the streets and with that so much if debate the science, cannot be relegated to the self-help manuals that were spread astoundingly at the end of last century, boarding this psychic condition. The attempt to rescue the discussion in the varied focuses, can perhaps be an initial step to recover concepts that were enucleated of our science, that every day, as we witness many times in our professional exercise, is defenseless and shaky, indifferent of the manuals conceptions, much more nearby of the banality and of immediate popularity, that they cannot be, in any way, confused for the ones of a modern science that is being built, like one of the humanity enterprising spirit valuable conquests. Of this legacy, cannot open hand.

5.4. A Modern Theory: Fields theory

> We watch amazed the rest invention for the representation; This man's new state, where the symbols conquer your place, the action their support reasons, the city constitutes around of the meditation and is defended by the organized action...The civilized life, whose invention refer to the Homeric poems, depends on a labor differentiation between infection kingdom and the superficial plan of the representation. (Herrmann, 1991a. pp. 108-109).

The Homeric illustration of the shield of Achilles exemplifies very well the origin, the purpose and the representation maintenance as a construct essentially human that leaves the man of his state of fusion of the things world, to build it as truly human. The shield can be imagined as owning two facsimiles. In its internal side would be represented the subject identity, as he recognizes, the representations constituted by the wish; the other side would be destined to represent the world rest, that we denominate reality.

The Psychoanalysis, like a human practice that refers to in essence to the man's humanization, a science and art among sciences, it seems to let contain in itself something characteristic of the Homeric inheritance.

Exactly Homer, the blind that anything saw, can see with the beauty of your poetry the exact moment in which the man humanizes, in which it lets the infection kingdom, of the effervescence and of indifferently of instincts, for in a rest, like a calm in full tempest, declaim your lineage, to what came and what represents, giving sense to himself and to your actions, that for more infected than are by love and by the hatred, they win meanings, organization and purpose.

Laid down in the couch, the patient with your suspended action, freely, like the warriors in your rest, wanders about yourself history, that for more different and distant of other your similar be, finishes showing your offspring of an unique matrix; In the warriors' case, Zeus; In the of the analyzing, your internal world, your renounced passions, your erected representations and maintained strongly by the belief in its legitimacy.

For your side, sat down sometimes comfortably, with your dispersed, floating attention, the analyst listens the one that lays down to his front declaiming your lineage, telling your history, in an almost unspeakable interval that is intervened to the daily fight, less ferocious than the Homeric battle, but, neither because of this less threatening, dangerous, under the clouds that threaten with the disorganization tempest, indifferently and of the coalition that annuls the identities.

Analyst and analyzing meet in a specific place, where the space, time are more than relative; The I, no, the past, the present, the future blend in a here and now; The field is created, sometimes similar to the ones of battle, because it is in it who intimate enemies meet. It is in this field, that the representations will be declaimed and will show your weakness, as well as the pretty Shield seized by Achilles, exhibited with pride, did not manage to protect your agile feet and neither it liberates him from their your destiny. In the field transfer, other so many shields will be seized many times with haughtiness, other with violence, other with suffering and weakness. Everybody will have in common to attempt to present only the coherent, the no contradictory, relegating to its edges just vestiges that it was proscribed, as well as real renounced wish and sequels small marks that stood out.

The analyst listens and, when it irregularly talks, its mark presence. It was present the whole time, but his communication seems strange and not directed to who, until then, related the epopee of your life. This listens of the analyst circles the shield borders, it finds the reminiscences that were abandoned and renounced, as well as, the "reasons" that made a things universe does not have been represented, or, represented of other different forms. His speech, given birth of this field that checked his listens, goes in him operate incisively to break the established field and to tease the beliefs set that even then I kept the identity, the auto-representation. The anguish and the pain are generated; the identity crisis establishes exposing the characteristics of field and of how it was articulated since its origin. The momentary disarticulation propitiates a special situation in the mental continent, in which a new fact can facilitate the structuring of a new field in which the representations can if settle. The identity crisis, the disarticulation, the field breaking needs for bearable of the chaos that is approached, a tolerance dose to the frustration, so to speak, necessary is done, so that other field is again articulated and new to presuppose maintain differently the representations.

When a new field is reestablished, the shields are again seized, however, again, the operation repeats and the new field will be broken, leaving on view "vulnerable, new heels crisis, other field... The interpretation, this "probe" that place by the space of the unconscious without a destination pre-determined, always emits new forms signals of psychic life, of other "worlds" to are discovered.

However, before the new worlds conquest, need every minute be signing our hands in the interior handle of our shield to sustains it firmly, need to believe in its effectiveness and, this belief, does us parade by the world outside with more or less dread, but believing in that in it is represented. The belief to keep up of the representation. The interpretation, this "traveler", shakes our beliefs enabling the exit of a restricted universe, as the dogmatic believer, in which everything is punishment sin and reason. It in the befitted to go for a beautiful voyage inside the human, until the prophecy, that is, life of each one accomplishes, with more or less glory.

An analyst can interpret, aided in the technique and in the theory, a work of art, a joke, a fact of the everyday, a literary work, an organization or group. Finally, the analyst does while it interprets, because it is the interpretation that characterizes the Psychoanalysis method and that gives you identity (Herrmann, 1991b; Meyer, 1993).

The psychoanalytical interpretation, like a particular case of interpretation, occupies a space highlighted in the psychoanalysis literature and practice. It inserts in its before same history of its constitution. In the works writings for Freud, such as, in the *Dreams Interpretation* (1900/1990) and in the *Psychopathology of the Everyday Life* (1901/1990), find a certain interpretative style that is advanced and if previous exhibition to the analytic properly told situation.

Constituted the analytic situation, it is established the field transferals. The interpretation, besides referring to that field, goes in it operate, breaking the set of presupposing in that patient's representations, of a group sustain, enabling a field rupture, exposing the properties, presuppose them of how it was constituted and opening the visualization possibility of how could if it structure in a new field, of how other representations could be built (Herrmann, 2001).

The interpretation arises, in the analytic context, based on field transfer established, of the mental game that is evidenced having roots in the wish, in the fantasy, in the delirium. "Is perhaps born, in last resort, from it the encounter of two beings desirous that wants want or not, work to four hands" (Figueira, 1988, p. 24).

In Meyer's thinks (1993), like method instrument, the interpretation would not limit to supply another (hidden) sense to the patient's speech, but to unveil the existence, presence and forms performance of psychic-not realized life, but as real and active as the ones that are under the perception domain. Serving to the method, driven to the field for him marked, the interpretation becomes an intervention have if, a practice challenging, inserts a Wedge in the compulsion to the repetition, imposing a difference and implying a divergence.

Finally, we could ask, for clearness effect: How would be the characteristic of psychoanalytical interpretation.

In your excellent liberate "Foundations of the Psychoanalytical Technique", Etchegoyen (1989) dedicates 10 chapters just to the Interpretation and one more chapter on the Aspects epistemologies of the psychoanalytical interpretation, for being the psychoanalytical essentially interpretative method. Clear that we remove today the interpretations tautological, in other words, the ones that find what they seek, or, yet, the ones that out of context, they apply to everything. All of them, more head product of interpreter than of the phenomenon or objectified fact.

Herrmann (1988, 1991a, 1991b, 1997, 1998, 1999, 2001) dedicated practically all its work and its life to the psychoanalysis method discussion, especially to the psychoanalytical interpretation. Your purpose, come in another, was the methodological depuration, trying to liberate the interpretative method of the consolidated theories, in which for vice of the technical, it could the interpretation be only a reflex, an effect of the preferential theories of a psychoanalyst.

Basing me preferentially in two of your works, *Psychoanalytical Clinic: the Interpretation Art* (1991a) and *Belief Psychoanalysis* (1998) will try to trace a small panorama of how the interpretation was understood and of its main function, in other words, the field rupture. The result of such formulations makes the psychoanalysis advances in your way of doing science and to integrate itself to other scientific disciplines, without because of this to give up your own method.

5.5. Interpretation and Representation: Field and Rupture

> We watch amazed the rest invention for the representation; This man's new state, where the symbols conquer your place, the action their support reasons, the city constitutes around of the meditation and is defended by the organized action...The civilized life, whose invention refer to the Homeric poems, depends on a labor differentiation between infection kingdom and the superficial plan of the representation. (Herrmann, 1991a, pp. 108-109).

The Homeric illustration of the shield of Achilles exemplifies very well the origin, the purpose and the representation maintenance as a construct essentially human that leaves the man of his state of fusion of the things world, to build it as truly human. The shield can be imagined as owning two facsimiles. In its internal side would be represented the subject identity, as he recognizes, the representations constituted by the wish; the other side would be destined to represent the world rest, that we denominate reality.

The Psychoanalysis, like a human practice that refers to in essence to the man's humanization, a science and art among sciences, it seems to let contain in itself something characteristic of the Homeric inheritance.

Exactly Homer, the blind that anything saw, can see with the beauty of your poetry the exact moment in which the man humanizes, in which it lets the infection kingdom, of the effervescence and of indifferently of instincts, for in a rest, like a calm in full tempest, declaim your lineage, to what came and what represents, giving sense to himself and to your actions, that for more infected than are by love and by the hatred, they win meanings, organization and purpose.

Laid down in the couch, the patient with your suspended action, freely, like the warriors in your rest, wanders about yourself history, that for more different and distant of other your similar be, finishes showing your offspring of an unique matrix; In the warriors' case, Zeus; In the of the analyzing, your internal world, your renounced passions, your erected representations and maintained strongly by the belief in its legitimacy.

For your side, sat down sometimes comfortably, with your dispersed, floating attention, the analyst listens the one that lays down to his front declaiming your lineage, telling your history, in an almost unspeakable interval that is intervened to the daily fight, less ferocious than the Homeric battle, but, neither because of this less threatening, dangerous, under the clouds that threaten with the disorganization tempest, indifferently and of the coalition that annuls the identities.

Analyst and analyzing meet in a specific place, where the space, time are more than relative; The I, no, the past, the present, the future blend in a here and now; The field is created, sometimes similar to the ones of battle, because it is in it who intimate enemies meet. It is in this field, that the representations will be declaimed and will show your weakness, as well as the pretty Shield seized by Achilles, exhibited with pride, did not manage to protect your agile feet and neither it liberates him from their your destiny. In the field transfer, other so many shields will be seized many times with haughtiness, other with violence, other with suffering and weakness. Everybody will have in common to attempt to present only the coherent, the no contradictory, relegating to its edges just vestiges that it was proscribed, as well as real renounced wish and sequels small marks that stood out.

The analyst listens and, when it irregularly talks, its mark presence. It was present the whole time, but his communication seems strange and not directed to who, until then, related the epopee of your life. This listens of the analyst circles the shield borders, it finds the reminiscences that were abandoned and renounced, as well as, the "reasons" that made a things universe does not have been represented, or, represented of other different forms. His speech, given birth of this field that checked his listens, goes in him operate incisively to break the established field and to tease the beliefs set that even then I kept the identity, the auto-representation. The anguish and the pain are generated; the identity crisis establishes exposing the characteristics of field and of how it was articulated since its origin. The momentary disarticulation propitiates a special situation in the mental continent, in which a new fact can facilitate the structuring of a new field in which the representations can if settle. The identity crisis, the disarticulation, the field breaking needs for bearable of the chaos that is approached, a tolerance dose to the frustration, so to speak, necessary is done, so that other field is again articulated and new to presuppose maintain differently the representations.

When a new field is reestablished, the shields are again seized, however, again, the operation repeats and the new field will be broken, leaving on view "vulnerable, new heels crisis, other field... The interpretation, this "probe" that place by the space of the unconscious without a destination pre-determined, always emits new forms signals of psychic life, of other "worlds" to are discovered.

However, before the new worlds conquest, need every minute be signing our hands in the interior handle of our shield to sustains it firmly, need to believe in its effectiveness and, this belief, does us parade by the world outside with more or less dread, but believing in that in it is represented. The belief to keep up of the representation. The interpretation, this "traveler", shakes our beliefs enabling the exit of a restricted universe, as the dogmatic believer, in which everything is punishment sin and reason. It in the befitted to go for a beautiful voyage inside the human, until the prophecy, that is, life of each one accomplishes, with more or less glory.

Chapter 6
The Psychological Clinic and Their Cases

6. The Psychological Clinic and its cases

The clinical cases are the touch stone of all therapeutic modality. Searching the theories verify that practically all originated in the scope of the clinical assistance. In the tell of Herrmann (1991), the theories almost always are born of the clinic and only are completely valid when they own clinical utility. The clinic can be considered a kind of theory thermometer. It is in the place where this creates, it transforms and it is many times overcome by new discoveries. When we attend our patient discoveries and formulations will go propitiating an accumulation of referring specific knowledge to him. If such knowledge can explain a whole class of present psychological phenomena in other patients, the generalization will have the statute of a true theory. Instead of to understand only a patient, interpreting him theoretically, applying a theory for each occasion, it passes to understand to others, to go transforming the understanding product in theory.

For Carvalho (2004), the human being can be considered a text the read being. Being this way, they should seek in it textual evidences and, to leave of them, embrace whatever has underlying and that promotes mobilizations of all order in the psyche surface, in other words, in the ego, the agent who enables the contact with the outer world. Thus, it should consider what this person made, as it did it and as tell have done to can advance in the procedures that take to the problems nature comprehension by means of interpretations, delineating the possibilities to execute your actions, and of the indications of conscious psychic and unconscious motivations in all behavior manifestations.

For Gabbard (1998), the psychotherapists that own a mind's vision psychodynamic understand their patients trying to determine what it is singular in each one, once these differentiate as a result of a history of singular life. It should understand the symptoms and behaviors just as the final common ways of subjective experiences, identifying the predominant value in the patient's internal world, their fantasies, dreams, fears, expectations, pulses, wishes, and self-images, perceptions of the other and psychological reactions to the symptoms.

Herrmann (2001), seeking an analogy with the machine of printing tissues, that as the mold prints determined standard, says that the wish is the matrix of the human emotions, that that give logic to the emotions of each person. It is as if the wish was a tissue woof with excess of us, with many of these us serving to maintain the united tissue. The others knots, the ones that are in excess, would constitute the traumas. When these knots are undone by the clinical work, by the interpretation, the psychic tissue is "untied", allowing the patient puts available to his conscious personality, their effective possibilities.

We can lead our daily life as if we in fact owned choice freedom, but, in fact, are limited, characters of a text written by the unconscious. Our loving choices, our professional interests and our leisure activities do not give by chance, but they are delineated by unconscious forces in a dynamic relation to each other (Brenner, 1969; Gabbard, 1998)

Tuckett (1993) considers a rarity find examples of clinical much related working, with details that it was told in the sessions. Such absence of detailed reports finishes, in fact, contrasting with the great number of discussions, besides about the technique that does affirmations of generic form.

In the continuity of your thought, Tuckett (1993) defends that the presentation detailed of clinical material covering assistance long periods could be very enlightening, because the experience, instead of generic theoretical discussions, could show in a clear manner the different forms of if lead a clinical case.

In opposite direction, Fig tree (1995) notes that all and any clinical material that is presented is resultant of a selection inevitable process for which there are not defined criteria and explicited, that define, like external parameters, what should make part, what should be included or not.

This discussion around of the form as the clinical case should be presented, especially in the psychoanalysis, raisin by a previous question, that arises, certainly, as a result of the discussion on the technique, that determines the ways by the which ones a clinical case should be led. It is around of the subjects that involve the technique that can notice the standardization great difficulty in the presentation of a case.

The psychotherapies psychodynamics history is harnessed to the initial development of the ideas of Freud. At the beginning, he got disappointed when realizing that the histories that your patients told about seductions suffered by relatives represented mere fantasies and not the truth, as it supposed. Freud built, to begin of these histories, all a framework etiologic that was, by the engagement with the truth scientific, destroyed and abandoned. Afterwards he discovered that the important was not the effectiveness of the environmental factor, but the affective reality of the unconscious fantasies, of the wishes that were repressed and dissociated of the ego.

After your new discoveries on the psychic operation, Freud (1996), in 1912, trying to systematize your technique, said that the technical rules that presented had been reached by your own experience along your years of working, concluding that it asseverated an appropriated technique to each individuality.

In "On the Beginning of the Treatment", Freud (1913/1996) presents the most including principles of your technique, especially when it suggests to the patient who that that this is going to say you differs of one talks common.

In a common talk the patient would try to keep a reasoning line along his observations, of your thoughts, excluding the intrusive ideas that could occur. It means, the patient, in one talks, would try to stay in the subject at issue, not letting it take by other divagations. In the therapeutic process, on the other side, the patient should tell everything that you came you to the head, should not give way to the criticisms, but to tell it in spite of them.

Afterwards, in *Constructions in Analysis* (1937), Freud (1996) establishes that the analytic work consists of two different parts, two separated places involving two people, had to each one their a different work. To the patient needs remember an experience that was repressed, and to the analyst goals discover, by the patient's memories, the symptoms and, in the repetitions, that that was forgetful. The hour and the way of revealing your constructions to the patient, as well as the explanations that can be offered, constitute the link among both parts of the therapeutic work, depending on the analytic work to bring to the light what was hidden, because hardly the psychic structure suffers integral destruction, especially when we care for psychic objects.

Of the technical point of view, just as theoretical illustration and just like always in the practice is observed, Freud, in this same work, differentiates the interpretation reconstruction, postulating that the interpretation would apply to something isolated of the patient material, just as an act fail, an association, and, the reconstruction gives when the therapist has his front a patient history fragment who was forgetful. We can deduce that the interpretation and the reconstruction are two different and complementary instruments of the therapeutic process, in which the interpretation would have the function of immediately working with patient's resistances and to turn possible the reconstructions assimilation, and these would embrace a layer of vaster and profound aspects.

Ferenczi (1919/1992) marks that all psychoanalytical method reposes exactly on this rule formulated by Freud, not doing any concession to the therapeutic session. However, the author affirms that the psychoanalyst does not have the right to of being sweet and indulgent or rude and rude, hoping that patient's psyche comes to be adapt to the characteristics of own therapist.

In *Neurosis and psychosis* (1924), Freud (1996) arises the hypothesis that these have source in the ego conflicts. More precisely, they would reflect a failure in the operation of the same, expressing itself in its difficulty conciliating all the exigencies that are done it. Such failure is in the tendencies relative intensity dependence in conflict and, to avoid a rupture in any direction, the ego can deform itself, subject itself the invasions of its own unit and to accomplish a cleavage of himself. In the last sixty years of the psychoanalysis history, the deformation suffered by the ego and its consequences in the personality formation was countless studies focus (Deutsch, 1942; Erikson, 1998; Klein, 1981; Spitz, 1979; Winnicott, 1975).

The main therapeutic goal, in short, is to turn conscious the contents that are met repressed and thus facilitate the expression adequate of the emotions. However several theoreticians have postulated other goals for the psychoanalysis, the basic elements of the technique keep until the present, and the obtainment of the main goal gives by means of a process that takes to the resistances decrease (Machado & Vasconcelos, 1998).

For Khan (1977), the therapist's task is not to be the mother, or transform itself in the patient mother, what, by signal, would be impossible. The therapist ought to, in determined cases, supply mother's functions, whose fault, during the development process, took to the distortion of many of the ego attributes of this patient.

Mental Diseases are not simple processes to understand or of if classify. Of the point of view psychodynamic can differentiate in them a primary process and another secondary, responsible for the disease. The primary process, or main nucleus of a certain disturb, can be conceived as an increased pulse, without voluntary control, that has as result the mental suffering, the anguish and a series of internal conflicts to ego. On the other hand, the secondary process of the illness it summarizes in the ego reactions in which are unchained, from need to control by part of this ego in the meaning of avoiding the displeasure, the anguish, the disturbing feeling that involve all the personality. In fact, we can think, practically all the semeiotics arises as a result of the fight between inhibition and the modification of some pulses, when the unconscious contents are impeded of arrive to the conscience and, as well as the affections, are impeded of expression through the motive discharge (Nunberg, 1989).

Not always the people who search psychological treatment are the ones that own serious psychic illnesses. It seems until the more serious is a personality upset, more intense also is the resistance in search psychological assistance.

People who suffer from some personality upset have its social very prejudiced life. The mental, in a way general upsets, can if present when a traces standard of characteristically inflexible personality, unadapted, significant cause implication or personal suffering to the patient. Once such traces constitute persistent standards of perception and of relationship with the environment and with itself, the personality upsets tend to turn be become long duration terms, difficult to face (Ebert, Loosen & Nurcombe, 2002).

What in the upsets is observed is an attempt to satisfy the needs without an adequate alteration in the external world, but, on the other side, of if you make an effort intrapsychic in the meaning of getting a change in the personal organization, autoplastic. Thus, the adaptation to the reality is pledged, varying in its implication degree. How much larger is its dismissal, larger also will be the consequences observed in the person's general operation.

For the theory psychodynamic, we can tell, in general lines, that through the exaggerated and intense utilization of some defense's mechanisms, a part of the ego was separated of its remaining and if fixed in satisfactions and inadequate reactions. We can think the larger part of the ego evaluates as threatening, the dangerous situations that, in fact, there are not anymore, than just are ghosts to frighten the personality at the present time, at person's present. How one of the consequences of this the attempts to influence directly these parts, that were separated of the ego, have little possibility to obtain success, because, as a result of the whole split process, just parts of the ego remain in touch with the reality, resulting in a weak ego, that has difficulties cooperating and to correspond adequately, for example, to a therapeutic process.

The personality functions general inhibition can be explained by the fact that the contents cannot remain excluded from the conscience by a defense's process accomplished only a unique time. On the contrary, to keep the defenses of constant form, the ego needs to spend force, energy of continuous way. For that continuous of spent energy, we call resistance. (Etchegoyen, 1989; Freud, 1923/1996; Menninger & Holzman, 1979).

One of the characteristics of all disturb is the one of establish a content and repetitive actions, a thought standard, an action standard. At this standard call compulsion to the repetition. It has source in the ID unconscious and fastens the pulses expressions standards. Such standards are essentially resistant to the modifications, and, most of the time, cannot be directly influenced, as we will see, in some clinical vignettes that will be presented.

For Freud (1912/1996), each person, through the joint action of its innate disposition and of the influences suffered during the first years, acquires an own method in the form how will be if lead and that will be tend during its life. If the need to love of a person is not adequately satisfied by the reality, this will tend to be approach of each new person that comes to know with expectations of accomplishing it. Thus, becomes comprehensible that loving investment who is partially unsatisfied, also it direct to the therapist person, because this will be put in a psychic series already formed by patient.

To this phenomenon Freud denominated of transfer, that in a first moment can appear as the most intense expression in the resistance, but that is become allied of the treatment when it has positive outlines, in which patient's confidence is deposited almost integrally in the therapist's illustration.

There are beginning experiences of the first childhood of which the person anything reminds for have been emphasized. The patient does not remind of absolutely anything, just acts, reproducing the experience memory, but as action, in other words, repeats it knows that it is repeating.

The patient, thus, in any therapeutic process, gives way to the pulse of repeating, that replaces the one of remember, not only in the therapeutic process, but in other activities and relations of your life, like standards impulses expressions. Such standards are, not rarely, very resistant to the changes, not managing to suffer direct influence. The patient unconsciously actualize the relationship past instead of remind it, propitiating to the therapist, thus, an information wealth concerning their passed relations. Just when the resistances elaboration is accomplished, what demands a difficult task for the patient, is just that the compulsion to the repetition, to the meaningless action, stops occurring in the therapeutic process and in the patient's life (Gabbard, 1998; Kernberg, 1995; Nunberg, 1989)

It belongs to your ego, not exactly in the conflict inexistence, that the personality depends to perform fully your functions. The harmony between the three personality instances, of the ID, of the ego and of superego, it depends on the synthetically function of the ego, in other words, of its capacity in mediate intrapsychic the several contents, as well as in manage the reality demands and the internal availabilities. There is always a latent conflict among personality instances that, however, remains silent while the ego mediation effectiveness keeps. However, such conflict can, without a doubt, become I manifest, if the synthetically function of the ego is by some weak reason.

The psychoanalysis defines for if constitute at the same time in a psychotherapy technique, a theory and a psyche investigation method. Such aspects are narrowly related and inseparable, because only can cure scientifically with an adequate technique and with a theory, so much of the technique as of the disease and of the psychological processes, in the measure in which we investigate what happens with the patients, and with an investigation method that coincides with the cure procedure, because, to the measure in which the person becomes to know to herself, it will be apt to modify its personality (Etchegoyen, 1989).

In Bleger's Vision (1992), the clinical psychoanalysis as well, for more strange than can seem, can be considered a laboratory method, whose enormous effectiveness as investigation procedure resides in the existence of a rigorous systematization of the technique, fundamentally based in the fixation of a framing, that consists in a limitation of the constant variables and in a certain variables control in each session moment. That control of variables occurs by the construction of an artificial situation, in which can have a rigorous observation of a session. The clinical method characterizes by a direct contact and investigator's folks with the studied person, contact that can extend to the main members of his half.

For Turato (2003), the study of case puts in the clinical methodology, because with he emphasizes the particularities of a phenomenon in terms of its sources and of its reason of being. It becomes a true model of the clinical-qualitative research that we propose to work with profound and intimate questions, like referring subjects to the disease, to the death, to the separation, to the personal relations, to the sexuality, to the ideologies, to the prejudices and to the patient's reality and our own positions.

So that a therapeutic process has continuity, so that a clinical case has its well off evolution, becomes necessary to the establishment possibility of a good *rapport* between patient and the therapist. Such condition can be favored when the patient owns parts of his preserved personality, such as the capacity of comprehending and of expressing your feeling, thoughts and emotions, even though these manifest in a way distorted and confused.

The therapy has as one of its goals eliminated the repressions or to weaken the defenses and to reproduce precisely those childhood old memories, whose repression stimulated the ego alterations. The therapy task can be successful just if get a modification in the ego attitude, an ego transformation regarding the material repressed of the ID.

Studying the clinical material of a point of view psychodynamic, the therapist can realize that the symptoms emerge of psychic conflicts, and that they are resultant of such conflicts. As we know, the neurotic symptom soothes the neurotic conflict. The symptom is formed by the ego forces interaction and of the ID. Through the therapy, psychic representations of the ID are put in discovered and, the opposite exigencies of the exposed ego. The analytic work undresses the layers of the psychic conflicts, exposing to the evaluation a layer after another, showing how we developed the symptoms.

In a way general, the psychological conflict absorbs much person's energy, letting the patient in an exhaustion state, passive before life facts, of the reality, and to without managing to modify the ambient in its return to obtain the necessary terms for the satisfaction of your wishes. On the other hand, when we have an adequate psychic operation, healthy, the systems present interconnected so that the synthetically function of the ego can do itself present. With the repression and the symptoms formation, the communication intersystem is interrupted and, thus, the synthetically function becomes a lot of failure.

It is through the repression and of the symptoms formation that some representations are separated of the affection to them pertinent. The representation becomes unconscious and the inhibited affection or, yet, linked to another representation. In other words, the personality it disorganizes, the reality is falsely understood, the impoverished thought and the complicated knowledge.

Mezan (2001), describing the functions of the repressive process, it argues that after a first action in which the repression separates the representation ideational affection load, it has yet, like task, eliminate the anguish, be projecting it in the phobic object, somatic the affection load, against-investing to the opposite psychic formations to the excluded representations and establishing the obsessive ceremonies. The symptomatic formation would give by this mechanism, giving source to the varied belonging clinical aspects to the neurosis.

A complication that arises for any process of psychic change is the fact that the pleasure principle persists for long time, as it affirmed Freud (1913/1996), like operation employee method by impulses sexual that are difficult to educate. Departing of these impulses, or of the ego, it gets put aside the reality principle. What if observe, therefore, is just that the changes cannot assist as a simple result of reflection and of the conscious consideration on the reality, because the symptoms are generated by different mechanisms: Or like formations in substitution of the emphasized forces or like conciliations between forces repressive and the emphasized, or still like reactive formations and safeguards against the emphasized forces.

The cure process becomes an assimilation process of the psychic possibilities, that formerly were remote of the ego by the defenses, assuring the continuity and the unit of the personality, what means, in other words, turn such apt ego to care for himself, to take care yourself (Khan, 1977).

But in what would consist the cure? It can be adequate to tell that cure symptoms means to turn them innocuous, unnecessary, in other words, submits them for treatment. Clear that certain self-control can be expected, as well as the healthy capacity of sending the control to the beans from time to time. Cure means care. The therapy cares for of the wish, it sends the patient to treat carefully his emotions, to recognize them the logic, to care for that it feels. Finally, we can think the cure in three heartfelt: The one of treat, the one of care for, the one of reach a reasonable point of complete.

The psychoanalysis, for Herrmann (2001), operates in a strange temporal register, in which acquisitions and new discoveries will go transforming the past, not the facts that in fact occurred, but its traumatic and pathogenic value, recreating patient's history and, through its, transform its present. An established dialectic where the transformed past modifies life at present and this, then, points to a future less emblematic, restricted by inhibitions, by fears without any value.

A clinical case frequently is written after its terminus or when the therapeutic process, in process, allows glimpsing a patient psychic life general panorama. Freud (1912/1996), did not advise accomplish scientific studies in a case while this is in process, because to gather its structure, obtain from time to time an up-to-date situation of how the case goes walking, predict its future progress, can take to a certain obliquity of the results. For him, the hit test conduct would be the one of the therapist can oscillate, according to the need, of a mental attitude for another, and just to submit the obtained material to a synthetic process of thought and organization after and only the case have been concluded. On the other side that we can imagine, Freud also did not advise to take notes during the analysis sessions, even though we had for goal the scientific publication of the case, because, for him, exact reports of analytic clinical histories are of smaller value than it could wait.

The course of the clinical case goes of the initial interviews at the end of the therapeutic process. The initial interviews enable patient history select knowledge, of their symptoms, inhibitions and the reasons that carried it to ask the intervention of a specialist. Its content does not limit to the information supplied concrete verbally by the patient, but it comprehends the way like this brings the material, their communications not-verbal and the attitude generally express in the narration, it expresses arrogance, isolate, if seductive, evasive, anxious exhibition etc.

Patient and therapist try anxiety in the initial interview, because if it treatment a new situation, ignored for both. The patient can manifest a wide repertoire of affections and feeling, as well as sadness, blame, shame, happiness. Your mental processes can be observed in terms of quantity, content, organization, idealizations and main identifications. The established communication should be patient personality significant and enlightening, enabling to this reveal far beyond of that that he knows about himself (Bleger, 1989; Mackinnon & Michels, 1992).

The initial interviews are particularly adequate for the activity diagnostic in which the therapist has the need to decide if the person who the search really requires some kind of assistance, which the kind of this assistance, and verify if the case that is presented is inside your technical possibilities. It is an action of knowing how to differentiated, in which we separate what it is own of the patient of that that is universal, discovering what it is you typical, the psychological configurations that compose it.

It is by means of a detailed interview that we observe the need to patient, besides, of being attended by another specialist and, when this present is done, suggest the necessary guiding. This does not imply in the assistance discontinuity, mostly when depression cases and of other mental upsets need an accompaniment of medicament.

The therapeutic process is initiated after the interviews, when it is established a hit among parts, that that we denominate of contract. It is in the contract that the mutual obligations are established, such as payment, frequency to the sessions, schedules and objective to be reached etc. Perhaps the most important in the contract be therapist's intellectual honesty, because anybody can honestly foresee accurately absolute that the future will bring. Should not promise cure or relief, but just to promise try to give some help to the patient with a technique that already showed effective for other people. In case the therapist does not wait, or do not foresee any progress for a specific case, the assistance not even should be initiated. The important is to evaluate the more adequate therapeutic approach and to accomplish the due guiding (Lindner, 1972; Menninger & Holzman, 1979).

Freud (1996), in *On the Beginning of the Treatment* (1913), compared the process psychotherapeutic to the chess game, in which any individual, when initiating your learning, soon realize that only the openings and the final of games admit a systematic and exhaustive presentation, once there is an infinite variety of plays that are developed after the game be initiated. As well as in the chess games, in that burrow to the therapy, find countless manuals that describe the beginning of the assistance process and its terminus, when and as this should occur. However, the middle of the game, what is going to elapse during the therapeutic process becomes impossible to of being foreseen, because the extraordinary amplitude of the involved psychic formations, the plasticity of all the mental processes and the wealth of determinate factors would be impossible to are all described, cataloged in advance as attempt of if works of the technique.

Established the contract, in which, as it was already told, they were defined the forms how is if work, the honorarium, the frequency to the sessions etc. had the development of the therapeutic process, with advances and backlashes, improvements and worsening, everyday occurrences and all a happenings universe that on he are going to happen. During all the prosecute the therapist and the patient should go evaluating, day after day, month after month, year after year, the clinical evolution of the case. As well as everything has a beginning, this process also will owe a day have an end.

The high should be combined, in the same way that the contract. The goal is to arrive to an ideal situation in which both the parts show satisfied, to a moment in which some pressures become alleviated, when the symptoms disappeared or became innocuous, giving place to an increasing welfare and to a relative independence, as well as to an enlarged tolerance side to revertible of life, to a better quality in the relation with its own I, to a notion of the personal history and integrity of the Me, with the relations consequent improvement with people, with the work and with the leisure.

6.1. Clinical Cases

Clinical case 1: Maria' Case

But as a clinical case develops? We can answer to that with the case that we will present to follow, suggested by the Prof. Dr. André Luis Jones in a round table, to be analyzed theoretically, in the University Braz Cubas.

Maria, teacher of a primary school, has 26 years and is single. She is tall, reasonably attractive, but a little obese. It has dark hairs and curious eyes. Her dress is simple, but of good quality.

She gives to impression that it could be more attractive than allows. Her tranquility and insecurity lack make her apparent to be younger than her chronological age. Maria developed a tense temperament and hyperactive. It talks about her problems with a dramatic preoccupation and if action of restless way.

During the initial interview, Maria gave to impression of being a cautious and shy person. I kept the low head and her curved shoulders. It looked sideways periodically for the interviewer and repaired meticulously in the room. It talked about herself hastily, as if a rest could cause larger anxiety yet. She was verbal and introspective.

The patient searched treatment because it felt depressed and unsatisfied with your relationships with the opposite sex, which ones invariably never lasted more than one year. At the moment was involved with a boy who knew there is already more or less a year and to proceed recently feeling the same symptoms of progressive dissatisfaction. Said that was worried constantly concerning about of her capacity of getting a satisfactory involvement, and it felt condemned to repeat the same behavior standard for all life.

Maria also complained about stomach aches, stains in the face and other organism dysfunctions, the ones she considered as psychosomatic. The doctors who consulted attributed these symptoms to the tensions of your everyday.

Recently, when we drove to the school, had one "strange sensation" that it would lose the control that was going to die or to be mutilated in an accident by car. She remembered have had the same sensation for the first time when it attended to a meeting marked with anybody from school that she did not know. In that occasion, she had feared that her boyfriend lost the automobile control and that both died. Since then that fear comes repeating itself periodically.

Maria's Life seems to be characterized by the control, constraint and wariness. When it expressed her dissatisfaction, she talked about the need that feels of following a routine ("I feel more certain of this way"), of plan her daily activities (she kept lists), and of deliberating carefully any action or new decision ("I take hours to buy a unique skirt"). She said that it feels blame most time, but does not know why. Your friends complain that sometimes she is "weighed" and does not have enthusiasm. She said that "it is difficult to relax and to let the things happen. Always feel as if it have to control me completely; I think I just am unable of have a good time me".

Maria said that was given very socially with people, that I had two friends and several colleagues. Regarding the women she always felt inferior and many times found "lost in the shade of them". In the masculine presence also felt anxious and inadequate. A characteristic worthy of note was her need to pet and if you dedicate for men that she actually did not find attractive. She avoided the interesting men" and gravitated in return of those that seemed "weak to after finishing the school, her meetings were little frequent. Her first sexual experience was at the age of 21. She felt conservative pleasure in the sexual relations, but it felt compelled and was envious of the pleasures that the friends told you. She did not have orgasm in the sexual relation, but it felt orgasm in the masturbation.

Regarding your family history, Maria has a sister three older years, from whom she felt distant when child. The father, a dentist, is seen as a "subject" without ambition that it could not breathe without mother's permission. In opposition, the mother, also teacher is seen as ambitious, overbearing and controller. She felt nearer of the father. It reminds of, when child, as unworried and playful while the mother was cautious, careful and severe. Maria it reminds of many funny experiences with the father, playing of free style wrestling, of provokes and to do tickles. When it reached the puberty, she felt compelled with the father, and soon it felt repudiated and disappointed with him. Maria said that your father is his dentist. It talked about the pain that felt when he worked on its teeth and in the apparent pleasure that that gave him. She reminds that it sometimes screamed of pain because of the drill obdurate and he played with her telling that I was a coward. Maria thought he "slaughtered" its mouth.

In the school life, Maria was well off academically and later came off well professionally. She has pride of this.

In the last five years she has, once in a while, the following dream: "I see the guy of a dog coming upwards of me with those enormous teeth and I me effort to awake. Is dreadful".

Comments:

In its commoner acceptation, the expression case design, for the therapist, the very particular interest that he dedicates to one of his patients. Most of the time, that interest takes to an exchange of your experience with colleagues (supervision, studies groups, etc), but, once in a while, give margin to an observation writing, that proceeds constituting then what we really call clinical case.

In the medicine the case remits to the anonymous subject that is representative of the disease, it talks, for example, of a meningitis case. In the psychoanalysis, on the other side, the case expresses being's singularity itself that suffers and of the speech that he directs us. This way, we define the case as the report of a singular experience, written by a therapist to attest his meeting with a patient and to back a certain advance theoretical.

After these preliminary considerations would like to stress that this patient was not attended by us, was not in psychoanalytical psychotherapy, and because of this what we intend to accomplish now is only an exercise, very limited, is true, but very illustrative.

With the goal of think of development of the clinical case, will present, to follow, a series of questions and answers.

What its explanation for the development of this case? What is important for the treatment?

–what wrong with for patient?

What if note is a very varied semeiotics, that is, at the same time to some main symptoms, that define in fact the personality structure and patient's psychic operation, observe other symptoms, that we could characterize as fruit, result of this psychic dynamics. The approximate diagnosis could be the one of hysteria, in nosology classical psychoanalytical, or next to the diagnosis of an anxiety upset, can like find in the DSM-IV. The hysteria characterizes for an increase in the excitation, marked by physical symptoms, like tension, tachycardia, fast heart rate and tremor, accompanied of apprehension, fear, obsessions or other similar feeling. The patient presents sexuality inhibition and a certain retracting affective, especially in that burrow to the relationships with the opposite sex, very unsatisfactory and without gratuity. Stomach aches, stains in the face, depression feeling" or even a certain generalized anguish express patient's apprehensions. One affect loosen, that we do not convert integrally in a somatic organization, to link itself for diffuse fears, besides a certain despair by the control loss, or a threat, that we represent as catastrophe threat, or more precisely, in the fear of the death, a way, so to speak, of denominate a despair, an internal anguish. Like characteristic trace of the hysterical personality, of a general way, find a certain not consummated excitability, that if manifest in her tense behavior, hyperactive, finally, your state of constant excitation. Their correlated, secondary symptoms of obsessive traces are apparently consequence of evitable of the blame, tension and provoked by superego, whenever a choice has of being taken, even though are to the purchase of a clothes piece, since your choices universe is infected by the prohibition Oedipal complex.

What made this if it manifested?

This dynamic, by the visa, was established from the existence oedipal complex, or, told from other way, in the not-completed of the existence oedipal complex.

Oedipal complex is central for the psychoanalysis with regard to the neurosis structuration. In the hysteria case, repressive, in a way general mechanisms, remove a pulse that tries to win expression, in the burrow to its satisfaction. Such pulse is repressed. But its repression does not mean that the pulse has died. This returns, of disguised form, like a substitute of the original wish, in symptom form.

We know very little of this patient, that for we is mere fiction. This way, from Maria's Report, but also using our imagination, conclude that its adolescence should also have been very disturbed.

In Oedipus complex case and of the woman sexuality is consensus that, so that a woman can become feminine, a long way should be running through. The girl, to reach its femininity, should change not only of sexual object, as well as of zone erogenous, pass of a sexuality clitoris, for the vaginal. Women, as the men, they are conceived as owning a penis (*phallus*). In the beginning of its life the girl has an existence after oedipal complex with the mother, phase in which to do not yet occur the sexual differentiation. The mother is who it cares for of the child, gives bath, burrow in your body, and excites it with their expensive. In this case, when the girl reaches the phase phallic, when your sexuality clitoris becomes intense, it realizes do not have penis and feels very prejudiced with that, since it imagines that everybody owns it. In this sense, the girl thinks it was prejudiced by someone. Someone took what she should own, and that someone only can be the mother itself. The child's psychology works more or less this way: If I have is because someone gave me, if I do not have is because anybody took me...Thus the mother becomes for responsible person for this misfortune, since it is with her who pass most time. Therefore, the girl approaches the father, coming in, so to speak, in Oedipus complex properly told. Clear is that, the father, somehow, will also go frustrate the child, and because it goes from encounter to the father searching that the mother did not give you, what also is an impossible task. For an evolution point of view positive solution at heterosexuality and the establishment of the feminine sexuality, the wish of a penis should be transformed in the general wish of a baby. At this moment is that the girl identifies with mother's feminine aspects, it cares for of your toys and of her dolls, or of the newer siblings. Just after it comes what we denominate of latency period that does not mean sexuality absence, but a certain preoccupations decrease and sexual activities. However, the existence oedipal complex will be able to suffer a retrocession, and the girl returns to the situation after oedipal complex, identifying or reaffirming a psychic position phallic. To be brief, the incestuous wishes in the Oedipus complex are repressed, and the barrier against the incest is built.

In Maria's Case, we observe a mother phallic that authority and a passive father that does not breathe without mother's orders. It seems to us, so, that Maria disappoints with that father and identifies in part with the mother phallic (she has mother's the same profession, what already it denotes a certain identification), what checks you a not feminine sexuality. This also could explain the distance that she maintained of the older sister that for displacement could be target of their desirous pulses of homosexual character. Your joy, afterwards, will not give with the men, in a heterosexual relation, but yes in the masturbation, that, fictional, can very well is a masturbation clitoris. The masturbation in itself is a rehearsal that occurs especially in the adolescence and that prepares the teenager for mature sexual life, however, itself, is an activity typically narcissistic and two times or homosexual, in which the one that masturbates has to fancy the pleasure of the another, the opposite sex pleasure, in case, in fact, the fantasy be to bisexual content.

Of Maria, little knows. We just suppose that these contents be present, since she rehearses relationships with men, even though these relationships are unsatisfactory, and despite her I manifest interest for weak men, go thus tell, little powerful. We think, by the data supplied in the report, is possible again imagine that her femininity was not definitively established, and that the sexuality be and have homosexual very strong pulses. Also they are repressed, what makes Maria exercises a constant vigilance about her.

Oedipus complex determines, by the identifications set that it provides to the child, their future choices. Nobody beat the foot telling that wants to be hetero, two times, three times, four times or five sexual. People finish as well as result of all a process.

Maria, did not manage to have a paternal image that inserted her in the heterosexuality, what in the posterior items will be vet of this case.

What would be the therapy goal?

Should enable itself to the patient a retaking of his existence Oedipus in the therapeutic relation, especially in the transfer field, so that the repressions are affronts and the pulse driven to the reality objects without prohibition, censures and free of the family infection. The therapy owes especially propitiate a certain change in the identifications established in the patient's psyche.

How to proceeds to it get that goal?

It was with the hysterical and obsessive that the psychoanalysis started. And by the fact of the same to can establish links transference, reviving in their transfer conflicts, the psychoanalysis also becomes indicated for that case, what does not exclude other therapeutic focuses.

Is important what is the patient have knowledge of the therapy? Until point and in which treatment apprenticeship?

It is not important for the therapeutic process that the patient has diagnosis hypothesis knowledge formulated by the therapist. That knowledge, after all, of anything would serve you, just would result, certainly, by the experience a hundred year of the psychoanalysis, in an increase of its resistance. In fact, the conflicts knowledge, that is, of the factors etiologic, should go becoming conscious as the resultant resistances of the repressions will go being expired. Thence, yes, that knowledge will have cure value, of transformation of something unconscious in conscious, enlarging thus the pulses conscious control fan by the ego, until then out of reach.

Freud said many times that the Psychoanalysis is a personality theory, a psychotherapy method and an instrument of scientific investigation, wanting to highlight that, for some special terms, intrinsically of this discipline, the investigation method coincides with the cure procedure, because, as the person knows to herself, can modify its personality, that is, can cure itself.

Which the treatment duration forecast? What would be the number of sessions?

With regard to the number of sessions, we can tell that the ideal is that there is the biggest possible number.

Compare the therapy with the learning of a foreign language. If you are going to study English once a week, it will have a certain time and a certain learning quality. However, if you have class your every day learning will be faster and of better quality. There is not a time limit in the psychoanalysis, as well as, in determined psychotherapies of psychoanalytical focus, differently of the brief psychotherapy, in which that time exists and is determined contractually. Should not promise what it is not sure of caning accomplished. Better then will be to let the process walks to then to evaluate all the situation, that for signal can modify itself, and too much, in the elapse of the therapeutic process.

Which ones themes or foreseen material what can arise during the treatment?

Practically all patient's history should bloom during the treatment. Its relation with the parents, with the boyfriend and girlfriend, your first diploma, the first bra, the menstruation, their sexual doubts, their dreams etc.

I saw. – Which ones patient's aspects would it is focalized? In which order?

Should be focalized all the aspects that are arising. The psychoanalysis bases its technique, on one side, in the patient's free association and, for another, in the free and floating attention of the analyst. The analyst, to form your judgment, does not base on an unique aspect, but in a their set that will go being deduced of that that the patient freely talks. In the measure in which such heartfelt will go configuring it, the analyst communicates them to the patient at the adequate moment. It is what we call interpretation. The interpretation should arise as association product, of the patient's psyche. Otherwise, we will have for tautology, that is, will put in it some content of ours, particular, of the set of our personality or of our personal or theoretical beliefs.

In the dream case of Maria what we see is something threatening, a threatening sexual relation "See the guy of a dog coming upwards of me". If we take literally, the "coming upwards of it configures me as a situation who will in fact stay for top, and it, so, will stay underneath. This illustration has dog the guy, with those enormous teeth... Something that it could not happen. The father, for signal was a dentist, was him who cared for of the patient teeth, he who with its drill obdurate machine (actually, perforator, because we perforate for then close) caused pleasure and pain, a prohibited pleasure, that it could not move away itself of the pain. The dream seemed to be a sexual relation with its own father, disguised.

We would like to note that the barrier against the incest is a human being's particularity; no other living being in the Earth side owns such prohibition. Because of this it is one wish injunction, worthy of censorship, even though are in dream.

The Dream Work tries to transform a sexual pulse of incestuous order in a dream. However, if the Dream failure Work, what observe is the anguish liberation, the nightmares properly dit, that awake the dreamer so that it recovers its defenses, that were fallacy.

Describe the relation nature between therapist and the patient. Which therapist's role? (Professor? Model? Neutral person? Another?)

The relation established between therapist and the patient runs away from a lot of the usual models. This relation has for base the transfer phenomena and of contra transfer.

The transfer refers to the update, in the therapeutic process, of feeling, attitudes and unconscious conducts, by the patient, that correspond the models that this established in the course of its development, especially in the interpersonal relation with its a little family, finally, constitutes the affective attitudes that the patient support and updates in the relation with the therapist.

Already in the contra-transfer can include all the phenomena that appear on the analyst, that emerge in him, and that constitute in fact a kind of therapist answer to the patient's unconscious manifestations, the effect that this has on the therapist. This way, in the psychoanalysis, the analyst is going to be transformed in the several imago that are going to arise according to the patient wish demands. He is going to be father, mother, confident, competent, donkey, professor, student, etc...In Maria's Case, the analyst will be, at the same time, the passive father, the father perforator, the dog, the sadist who does her suffer, the mother phallic that to all breathlessness and that so much envy cause to the patient, etc...

We would like to stress that how much larger go to the repetition in the situation transfer, freer to become the patient of his conflicts. The psychoanalytical process will propitiate that the patient experienced, by the speech, the original situation of the conflict, of their inhibitions, of their symptoms, could, thus, along time, have your free life daily of the inhibitions, of the symptomatic apparently meaningless situations. In the present case the therapist, through the patient's repetition, will be witnessing, inside, Maria's History and, from this privileged place, can interprets it of effective form, giving new meaning to their acts, diluting what it is not you necessary.

What changes can hope that they occur in the patient as a result of a well off treatment?

The criterion used by the World Organization of Health to designate a healthy life does not base on presence or not of symptoms. For example, someone can have a liver cancer, without having any symptom and that does not mean that it to do not be sick. Other people can live for a long time, and with life quality, even with chronic symptoms that would not limit its activities. This way, the presence or not of some symptoms, in the modern conception, does not mean that a person is more or less sick.

In principle patient's relation with the therapist goes letting of being, it goes losing the character transfer, becoming more realistic. The therapist goes passing the seen being and sense as a person, letting of being target of massive projections of the relations from both. The interpretations become integrated most to the patient's daily, without causing strangeness. The patient precedes the meaning of his actions, without fright, since he knows a lot. It manages to foresee their actions, it plans them and to act of rational form when you thus befit you – what I was not Maria's Case, who practiced acts compulsively - as well as, it will be able to have the necessary confidence to be able to send the control to the beans, because there is not anymore that basic insecurity, that unnamable fear. Only can lose the control who owns it, what was not Maria's Case, who I kept the vigilance about her to be dominated by uncontrollable pulses.

With the treatment the patient becomes able to work better with his internal and external problems, when it occurs a certain symptoms ceasing or a better tolerance to the same. In the case at issue, for example, Maria could still feel a right timidity before the men, insufficient, however, to take her to prohibit herself of having relations and to obtain loving, lasting, free gratuities of limiting anguishes.

It waits, as well, with the treatment, a better integration and relation with its own I, in other words, a larger freedom feeling (is worth remind that Maria felt compelled, cautious), a capacity of obtaining more happiness and a tendencies decrease to the depression (Maria also felt "depressed"), besides a significant change in the relation with the others, that is, with the parents, friends, spouse, etc. In the Maria's Case would be also expected occur a certain progress in love object relations, in the direction of a representatives' choice objects not incestuous that can satisfy their needs to companionship, reciprocal love, maternity and mutual support. This way, a "des-contamination" incestuous in her family relations could give source to a more effective approach with the sister, with the father and with the mother.

Another aspect the considered being refers to the changes possibilities in their relations with the ideas and the things, with the goal of improving the interest by work, of proceed the professional satisfaction as an end in itself and a way for an end, taking to a larger ability and efficiency in the activities, as well as toot par possibility ludicrous activities with a minimum feeling of blame. There are people who go on holiday and keep blaming itself for take part the same; Worried, do not relax. Maria felt blame most time, did not manage to relax.

One of the more important aspects for the high of a patient is the acquisition of a better capacity to support the failure and the frustration. Since neither only of success lives the man, the failure, the frustration and the pain always will be present in life of anybody, being inherent to when being alive.

The psychoanalysis does not transform the patient in other person. It offers terms for the psychic development, so that the patient reaches that that is you own, within their possibilities, and that it, for him, would have reached, in case internal and external circumstances did not have had effects impeded. In different circumstances Maria perhaps had all the terms to reach her integrity while person, while woman, while worthy human being of a fuller life, of live and to do not be lived, until her life if it accomplished, with larger or smaller glory.

How it is determined and decided the treatment end?

According to the criteria previously explicitly, analyst and patient owe close to establish the analysis terminus. It is interesting note that after agreeing the raising, it occurs a certain repetition, in a time's brief interval, of the history passed by the patient in the own analysis, what can deceive the inexperienced therapist, thinking the patient is worsening. It will be just reviving its history.

Such circumstances would be the thermometer of a well off analysis, especially, when the patient remembers the analyst as a person who rendered you a good work, without debt or longing sentiment.

There are different theoretical lines used in the clinical practice, generating different styles. In the sequence will proceed exposing some of them, extracted of the literature, that will be able to be very elucidative.

Clinical Case 2: The Scratch

The case to follow was described by Herrmann (1991, P. 173), in the Clinical Psychoanalytical: *Interpretation Art*:

A patient it scratches. It plucks skin pieces, of the back, of the arms, of the head. Invaded, the analyst for times scratches, in resonance, the corresponding zones of his own body. It is this therapist's first inclusion in the symptomatic, perhaps the least serious hell. It occurs a dream: For patient sustains in the arms a girl, cover of hurt littlies, of which someone withdraws carefully the peels; under these there are sanguinary points. The feeling belongs to disgust and of affliction.

It is possible to comprehend that between patient and analyst is sustained an infantile patient, hurt, whose protections the interpretation withdraws carefully, when it clarifies the result of auto-aggression. Peeled, they remain hurting opened. A failure is imputed with justice to the interpretations: However correct in the anguish apprehension, do not manage to close the space between "Me who is scratching" and the "I that is scratched", scrub the own skin. There is here a neurosis subject subtle partition. Of a side the symptom conversion reaction, from other the conscious measures to mitigates it, that, as almost always in the neurosis, finish for accomplishing the same unconscious purpose to what tried to oppose, because to scratch it itself produce more itch. The psychoanalytical interpretations, in this case as in so many another, allies almost naturally to the measures egotistical that aim to combat the symptom, without realizing that the symptom and the ego collaborate in the same conflict expression, forming a vicious circle. The analyst's interpretations scratch for patient, with effect, decreasing momentarily her anguish, but, as all scratch, even produce itch, or until wounds, is what it teaches the dream. What hurt and in which skin? What there is between conflict impulses and the protective measures of the ego or else the identity and reality representations surface? The representations set of this patient form a kind of world-map, projected in its coetaneous surface. Of each skin side, tell, there is a nail to scratch: The nail of inside, under the skin, is the own itch, the symptom, and the nail of outside and to scratch it itself, the ego that reinforces that to what intends to oppose itself. It tells for patient, in certain moment, that a dear friend traveled. In the good-bye, she tells you: "You are for responsible person for my itch, with her travel, is for her cause…" Under the slogan "the world in my skin", our customer controls all the relations; she scratches them by parts, systematically, in the epidermis. "Now I am her scratching in me, unfaithful friend", could be telling.

The specific intolerance to the distance and to the independence, in the neurosis, will be our first lesson in this case. It addresses neurotic aggressiveness specifically against such categories linked to the separation, reproducing with its monotony denial. The space designated to other is reduced to a depth minimum, to the epidermical surface, like result the identity skin of the neurotic it alienates, it loses itself when the other moves away, or it at least scratches in the loneliness. Already the aggressive answer, the scratch itself, physical or spiritually, is a control attempt on the another, captured in the neurosis body surface, control that if lack of control then and even exacerbates pruritus of the absence incorporated by force and in incensed annoyance (…) In a word, the interpretation would owe softly let scratches – as if he would say "letting it arises" -, of the interior outside, the hidden wish, for take it! It strongly in hands when he shows itself, expressing your drawing with clearness and economy. At a certain point, a memory comes to elucidate part of the itch time meaning and calms a little for patient. "My mother told me that, small, when it did me wait I scratched myself". For certain time, she if fall tranquility. The interval between scratch and to scratch it itself, that the interpretations did not hamper, was performed by a souvenir. Memory: Time back that bring the absent mother.

However time of wait, time forward, reopens the skin wounds and of the soul; the scratch itself attempts time abolition of waits – for patient it scratches a lot in the waiting room and in all life waits. This temporal dichotomy is common in the hysterical neurosis: Time back, time of longing, it enriches by the time emptying forward, time of the human contact and of life construction. The wait denial, symptomatic temporal form elect by the patient, constitutes a sense of irritated time's, prurience, that finishes for embodying all your daily, but that is in force especially in time of the neurosis. Itch Monday lesson: Time is expects denied, it expects is hurt (narcissistic), while the controller reproduction of time, through memory and reverie, is alike to when scratching itself, evoking fugally the wished scene, recreates continually the same tension that tried to eliminate. I call the attention, finally, for the intervention of a colleague, when of the first exhibition of this material. Sustained him who scratches it I resulted from, for derivation, of the cry, when the mother was absent, during the childhood. It can be true. However, the temporal-space regime of the scratch, her circular self-induction, prurience double nail provoker, the skin map, the irritating position of the interpretation, would lose all this its specificity, if we adhered hastily to any translation reductionism. If a day for patient comes to cry and to stop scratching itself, the clinic spirit will agree of good well with such kind of net genetics, very vulgar in our psychoanalytical thought. For now we stay with the itch theory. All child cries, all patient complains. They are non-specific forms of aggressiveness. To comprehend however the neurotic aggressiveness is better let their specific constitutions penetrate us, through the logic of a concrete symptom that speculates in direction the common hypotheses. It is necessary to feel from other the pain in the meat, in the skin at least.

As can notice in the synthesis of the case presented above, Herrmann proposes a clear strategy, in other words, immerse and to let they arise patient's psychic configurations for take it! Those in consideration, without resorting to the method fictive of simply translate theoretically the presented symptoms. Thus, the psychoanalysis, in each specific clinical case, it goes clarify in particular and individuality of each, what there is of universal in all human beings.

Clinical Case 3: CID 10

In the Classification of Mental Disturbs and of Behavior of CID – 10: Clinical cases of Adults (OMS, 1998), find cases collected clinical practically of the whole world. All of them follow a certain presentation standard, not in the treatment meaning itself, but, just, for conduct ends and of diagnosis.

The script in general found in practically all the related cases consists 1 – in the **patient's presentation** (name, age, profession, marital status etc.), 2 - in the **presented problem** (facts happened, current symptoms and passed, as it arrived to the assistance service), 3 – in the **history** (with patient's general data on the childhood, adolescence, marriage, professional performance etc), 4 - in the **discoveries** (signals and presented symptoms), 5 – in the discussion the, with the respective diagnosis.

To exemplify this presentation form of clinical case, we choose a, that we consider emblematic.

Presentation: Ayse is an Egyptian of 27 years, married and without sons. It is nurse in a maternal-infantile clinic in Alexandria.

Problem: Ayse was led to the psychiatric hospital by the husband because it was very excited and talkative. After a discussion with the husband, four days before, Ayse left furiously of home and was to the mosque, where it remained all by night praying. When it came home by morning, your husband, bored, said him that was wanted to pass all by night in the mosque, should go to live there. After the fight she changed for mother's house, where it started to get more and more disturbed. Very shaken did not manage to sleep, it talked almost incessantly and it refused to eat. Ayse recited prayers fervently, although it mixed some of the words, without realize apparently this. Her endless talk was mostly about religion, interrupting it just to recite prayers, in which accused countless people of being sinners, ordering them that prayed. The mother called the husband of Ayse and said him that she was your responsibility. Ayse refused treatment, and then your husband carried the force for hospital.

History: This was the second Ayse's Marriage and occurred two years before the current problem. Your husband, of 34 years, was a very devote Mussulman that worked on a factory by automobiles. They did not have sons and this provoked tension in the marriage. Your first marriage, at the age of 21, just lasted some months because the husband was to work on a neighboring country and she did not see it neither it heard of since then. At that time of the internment of Ayse in hospital her father had 54 years and her mother 56. Ayse was the Thursday daughter of a family of two siblings and six brothers.

Ayse had developed great interest for religion when child. From the seven years wanted to learn Koran, decorating most book. She had a beautiful voice and was frequently invited to sing in social events. It was a sociable person that found easy to do friends, appreciating the fact that your ability to sing – and also to dance – turned frequently her attentions center. She was an active woman and generally optimistic, although it admitted feeling depressed sometimes. There was no history of mental disease in her family.

At the age of 22, Ayse had a depression long episode after the dissolution of her first marriage. She felt melancholic, with self-confidence loss; it isolated and it did not want to sing or go to parties. I had difficulties sleeping; it awoke early and felt tired; It lost appetite and weight. It got however keep your job, with just some few occasional days of license for disease. She did not look for a doctor. After about six months she gradually improved and recovered her activity habitual humor and level.

Discoveries: In the internment, Ayse had exhibited, for four days, an irritable and expansible humor, with loquacity, hyperactivity agitation, sleep and grandiosity lack of delirious character. No psychopathic symptom was observed. There was no evidence of any organic etiology, neither hyperthyroidism signal. It was not suspected substance psychoactive use. The current episode satisfies, therefore, to the symptomatic criteria for habit without psychopathic symptoms (F30.1). The gravity allows the qualification for this diagnosis, although the duration is of less of a week, because it was necessary hospitable internment. There was an affective episode, in the past, of depression takes to moderate. Your diagnosis, therefore, is: Bipolar affective upset, manic current episode without psychopathic symptoms (F31.1, OMS, 1998).

As if can observe the case does not present the form as for patient was attended, like the interviews were accomplished; It constitutes only a several interviews product by the which ones for patient maybe passed, besides the observation of her psychic state and behavioral manifestations during for hospitalization.

Clinical Case 4: The Big Proof

The Education Department and Culture comes promoting the National Exam of Courses, the famous Big-Proof, with the goal of evaluating the teaching offered to the students by the faculties. What has been observing in the last proofs is that, in the Psychology area, this evaluation is always made from the presentation of a clinical case for analysis. We consider thus important, in this article, that care for clinical cases, present one of them, the of the Big-Proof of 2001.

You were summoned to examine the case of a patient put into hospital in the psychiatry division of a hospital. It is Saulo, a youth 15 year, with typical inquietudes of adolescence that tried suicide cutting your pulse arm until the elbow. That happened soon after to a sporty event in the new school, when it felt have disappointed the people with his bad performance, exactly when it made an effort to do friends. After of this, it transformed in a "dreamer", change apparently realized by the members of your family, however anybody has spoken anything about the subject with him. Was then that tried the suicide, and it certainly would die if did not have been found by one of your siblings. After put into hospital weeks seemed better. It was affectionate to the professionals that had been rested by him and that medicated it with antidepressant. His dreamy way was considered an unequivocal signal of clinical depression. After a month had high, but soon it returned, after other serious attempts of suicide, that the patient justified for feeling that I had embarrassed your family with the previous attempt.

It should notice that the contact with the patient in hospital was surprising: be a question of a nice, athletic youth, with a healthy, well, dressed appearance and capable to conduct as if anything was abnormal in her recent history, however it had a terrible scar in your arm. It was notorious that the family of Saulo did not have made an effort in any mental work to work with the anguish of this dramatic situation. The parents of Saulo were affable people, but superficial. The mother was an efficient housewife and the father, a successful liberal professional. They were in a good financial situation. They were oppressors neither cruel nor passed a lot of time with the three sons, always involved with sporty activities. However, were not able of sit down with the boy to express his feeling and to argue any of your problems. They were not willing people to reflection. The family, as many of this kind, seemed ideal. Its slogan: "Everything is going to if transform for better". Were considered by their friends and neighboring stable people, with the feet in the ground. For all of them, Saulo's Fact try to kill was incredible and outside the limits of the common sense. It was something that it could not be taken seriously and should be capable like an unhappy episode, which Saulo would go to overcome, because "the strong people let the things back".

1. How you comprehend Saulo's crisis, that is, what are your clinical hypotheses concerning what motivated his?

2. According to line theoretician-clinic of your choice, which you're proposed of guiding of this case? Justify it.

These would be our answers:

1. Saulo, young of 15 years meets, as it is related us, in the adolescence phase, with your typical inquietudes, in other words, as it understands the psychoanalytical theory, in an evolutionary phase during which the person establishes her adult identity. An important moment that contains all a maturity process. It is in the adolescence that is going to occur the definitive dismissal of the objects of infantile love and, so that this happens, the wishes oedipal and your concomitant conflicts come back to arise. That interior breaking with the past shakes strongly teenager's emotional life, once to when opening new horizons and arise not just new hope, but also, anguish and fear.

It is in the adolescence that the ego ideal comes to be constituted as a superego, resultant of the Oedipus complex wide outcome. It constitutes a formation intrapsychic; relatively autonomous that serves of reference to the ego to appreciate your effective achievements, a special psychic instance of censure and of self-observation.

Saulo seems to do not have corresponded to his ego ideal, considering him a failed, and the result was a shock in your self-esteem. This shock in the self-esteem and the self-confidence consequent reduction are primordial symptoms found in the depressive state that, for signal, is the clinical diagnosis accomplished by the professionals who medicated it.

The parents of Saulo in spite not being oppressors and neither cruel, they seemed to be indifferent to anguishes, washings, to your son's weaknesses and a mortal, harnessed indifference to an exigency of natural success of the strong. Their parents they related with the sons through sporty activities, and does not belong to if it find strange that Saulo revealed his internal crisis (suicide attempt) after feeling failed exactly soon after to a sporty happening. The who then disappointed, or else, whereby saw up to now, for these illustrations internalize, demanding?

About the adolescence remains argue that for psychopathology installs when the teenager if fixed in solutions narcissistic, taking refuges himself in the isolation and in the fantasy, in which the omnipotence and the idealization, many times of the destruction, occupy the central role. It remains us, so, mark that Saulo, before the suicide attempt, there was if transformed in a dreamer, indicative of a worthy adolescence of special clinical attention, in which the teenager feels fail before the tasks that is proposed to accomplish.

2. We also can consider that the motivation for the apparently irrational act of take life can be considered itself like a dramatic attempt of communication, since such gesture suicide it repeated as soon as Saulo returned to his house. Such suicidal gestures, they tend to repeat itself when the communication purpose does not obtain success, as there is it very knows in the psychiatry, many times taking the subject, in fact, to the death. For the family of Saulo, the suicide attempt should not be taken seriously, but qualified as a simple unhappy episode, thing that reinforces our hypothesis on the suicide attempt significance.

We would argue with the professionals who medicated it and we would suggest sending Saulo for teenagers' Psychoanalytical Psychotherapy, because, as can ascertain, Saulo is not managing to pass by this development phase without aid, with the adolescence crisis taking a pathological configuration.

Finally, for being the capital important family for the process teenager would ask an interview with the parents of Saulo, not only to clarify them about your son's situation, as well as to sensitize them, if possible, to seek psychological aid through couple's psychoanalytical psychotherapy or of family.

In fact, brief relates of clinical cases presented by Big Proof demand, for its solution, that the person has the clinical thought developed in some theoretical approach and that also owns a reasonable notion about which the best conduct the followed being. The goal, in short, is the student formation evaluation in some approach, because your answers will depend on the chosen approach and of the theory application of his preference.

For Gabbard (1998), psychodynamic principles are of great importance, even in the upsets treatment of biologically based behavior, because the therapies frequently used to treat them are full most of the time of significances, and without a vision psychodynamic of the involved phenomena, would not have how to explain or to lead better the case.

Clinical Case 5: Organic Implication

We extract a clinical vignette, of a case with organic implication of the beautiful Gabbard's Book (1998, P. 33-34), *Psychiatry psychodynamic*.

You was her a single man of 29 years old with TOC. At the moment in which it presented for psychiatric hospitalization, it related a history of 10 years of obsessive-compulsive symptoms and complained about being totally captured at home in the last eight years due to the grotesque, terrible thoughts" and incapacitated that never ceased. Eight years before the admission, when the Mr. To became to do not leave anymore of home, your mother it retired, could cares for him and to satisfy your enema demands. Life of her rotated around of him.

The Mr. A. was confused from need to avoid contamination of any species. Also worried with the possibility to render pregnant some woman, because it feared to have semen in hands. Therefore, it became a hands compulsive washer. It insisted that your mother remained with him 24 hours a day. Although she did not sleep or took bath with him, assisted him to dress himself, so that he did not need to touch his clothes, preventing thus the contamination. He also asked that she followed an elaborated ritual, with 58 steps, to cook his meal and to put it at the table. In case did not follow the ritual accurately she had to discard all the meal and to initiate again the whole process. She had to if undone of thousands of dollars in food every year, in order to answer to these demands. The Mr. A. also insisted that his father should remain out of home or in other comfortable, so that there was not the risk of being contaminated by the germs that the father brought from the work.

The infantile development of the Mr. A. did not present notable aspects, however he remembered a very unpleasant episode when I had about five years old. It reminded having seen the father grabbing his mother by the breasts, while she screamed that the patient helped her. He tried to prevent his father of continuing; however it was supplanted by the man's older force. It remembered of having if heartfelt terribly badly concerning the incident and cried realize himself unable of save your mother.

However A. Mr. has gone to several psychiatrists always refused to return after the first visit. Certain time agreed to take clomipramine; however it interrupted the treatment after the first dose, alleging discomfiture with side effects. Their parents realized that they finally would have to hospitalize him, because we were disabled. When it arrived to hospital, the doctor asked him because it searched treatment. He answered "I am determined to be dependent – mean, independent". The doctor commented the fact that firstly he had told "dependent", and it asked: "There is perhaps some part in you who would it like to remain dependent? The Mr. A. answered: "You refer to my mother?" "The doctor answered that he should know the answer best than he. The Mr. A. reflected for a moment and said:" Well, she cares for very well of me".

The Mr. lapse A. provided a glimpse of the unconscious motivations of this resistance to the treatment. Any kind of well off treatment threatened your dependence relation with the mother. If for clomipramine had possibility to help him, then he would not take her. Similarity, he would invalidate any other treatment ambulatory efforts or hospitable.

After about a hospitalization week, the Mr. A. defied members' team expectations. It preceded presenting dramatic improvements. It managed to touch handles without fearing the contamination; it could read magazines that other had touched, besides having reduced considerably time expense with the wash of your hands. This improves occurred without the medication use. The Mr. A. commented that was felt "well less nervous" in hospital that it had imagined. Conforms we explored how much the hospitable environment had reduced your anxiety, it became apparent his increasing preoccupation with your sexual wishes regarding the mother. It commented that when his mother dressed it, it felt "something sexual". The environment dismissal emotionally loaded of its house turned less problematic his aggressive wishes of keep your father far from her, became less disturbers. Due to the decrease of your anxiety concerning their sexual and aggressive wishes, their obsessive-compulsive symptoms were not so necessary to contain its anxiety.

For Gabbard (1998), the presented case illustrates of clear way the interface between psychodynamic and the biological. Although the obsessive-compulsive symptoms could have a biological source, they reveal one wish symbolic of conquer the maternal affection in your father's detriment, like illustrated by their infantile memory. In other words, their wishes oedipal regarding the mother and the compulsive rites acted like a defense against such wishes, consuming all your time with the symptoms. The comprehension psychodynamic of his resistance in take the prescribed medication and to the treatments in general, it was of vanishes importance so that A. Mr. came to cooperate with the treatment, because your resistance meant that any improvement of his symptoms would imply in the loss of your position privileged regarding his mother. Their symptoms, as could observe, got, in fact, remove the father of his house, separating the couple and enabling with that the accomplishment of your infantile wish, with a mixed of hatred and of eroticism, characteristic these present in Oedipus complex nucleus.

Fenichel (1981) considers Oedipus complex the culminating point of the infantile sexuality. The development erogenous goes of the oral eroticism until for geniality, could be conceived as a set organized of loving and hostile wishes, and lived with the maxim intensity in the phase phallic of the development sexual psychic, with your decline demarcating child's entrance in latency period. It suffers a reviviscence in the puberty and can be overcome with relative success, besides determining a particular kind of loving choice.

For elimination of the wishes oedipal in the adult life represents the normality prerequisite, while the unconscious fixation to the oedipal tendencies characterizes the neurotic mind. The psychoanalysis considers Oedipus complex as a fundamental factor in the personality structuration and in the orientation of the human wish, psychopathology main reference axis psychoanalytical (Fenichel, 1981; Freud, 1909/1996; Laplanche & Pontalis, 1983).

Clinical Case 6: The Rape

The example that follows was extracted of Master dissertation by Raquel Ap. Spaziani (2004), defended in the Pontificate Catholic University of São Paulo, Guided by Prof. Dr. Fabio Herrmann and Co-orienting and Clinical supervised Prof. Dr. Claudio Garcia Capitão.

To the first interview marked with the parents, in February 1990, only the mother, Lady Maria, attended, alleging that the husband did not want to come, because does not manage to talk to anybody about the occurred with the daughter. According to her, "he nowadays only knows how to drink". Isadora was rape victim. It is now newspaper headline. The columns policemen cuttings they find spread on the desk close to which conforming Lady Maria.(...) The mother cries a lot and little manages to talk about her daughter. That to who it refers to is now only a girl who does not recognize most – a raped girl. "A shame for me, I did not have anything that send her alone to buy foolscap," tells the mother.(...) They were more or less nine hours in the night when Isadora had come home. "Just to look at her already knew what I had happened, she was very white and cold, in her legs the blood drained". The girl was taken to a hospital where received the first helps and was submitted to a surgery for intestine rebuilding. I hardly had passed the anesthesia effect the mother asked you: "Why you came in the young man's car, daughter?" The girl answered then has been put by force inside the car and that I had suffered threats.

The first interview with Isadora occurred in February 1990. When I presented me her in the clinic reception and invited her to come in the consultation room, she smiled and accompanied me. I said you that it could choose a place to stay, and she soon answered: - "For me anywhere is good". Isadora it sat down, curved shoulders, look sad. I asked knew what it did there and she answered quickly: - "My mother said me that you are going to take the pain of my heart. It explains me that the heart hurts whenever it reminds "of that that the young man made". It is as soon as since the first session and along almost the whole therapeutic process she is going to refer to the rape. When it mentions the rape is panting and shrinks, in a gesture that demonstrates much fear, in an attitude from whom is reared.

Tell that did not like other psychologist, because he keep doing questions about "that that the young man made" and she does not like talking of this with anybody. Also tells have meaning fear of the psychologist when a day he hugged her if to fire. Thus, Isadora told soon in our first meeting as expected anything of explicit questions about the rape be treated(...) The first drawing accomplished in the first session was the drawing of a rose that I had, according to her, two years; Nobody had her planted, the wind had loaded the seed. It was a happy rose that was in the middle of a forest with other pink friends, and it was cared for by time. Isadora demonstrated thus the wish to resume time in which the sexual aggression still there was not if become real and was happy, since after "of that that the young man made" did not feel anymore lady of the destiny. It was now loaded by the wind, with uncertain destiny. It could be perhaps a beautiful drawing – a gift for the therapist.(...) It did another drawing that represented its family, to which gave the title

"Ride in the Park". Started the drawing by she herself on top of a stone, what let her greater than the parents, pointing me as well as she felt – a child having to grow too fast. The father, for perhaps having been the one that did not protect her, was the last the suspended drawn being, without the line that represented the soil. It can indicate the way as Isadora realizes the father after the rape, "pretending that anything had happened: He "never burrows in this subject". The oldest brother also was drawn suspended, without support, but when it finished the drawing and realized this detail, it drew what told be a stair, under the illustration that represented the brother. In the drawing of your family Isadora also made a tree in the middle of the paper sheet, staying thus, she and the siblings separated of the parents (...)

In the session next narrated that your older brother has been going to Church "just because it has a siblings' equal suit". And I asked: "And the women? As if they dress to it go to church?" It answered: "Of skirt, pants cannot of appearance any". Looked at her accomplished pants - she had told me when arriving that it was coming back of to Church –

She laughed and told:

Hein! I am child yet. Although already I need start to go of skirt, but you still are child, said – you the therapist. "Is just that soon already am going to it do 11 years, do not be anymore child. It knew that I do not have anymore nightmares? After came here that day, never more dreamt bad things, only have good dreams!", and it opened the arms to speak about the good dreams.

I investigated if she wanted to tell me the good dreams and she said if do not remind. Then I asked about the nightmares and Isadora clarified me do not have nightmares. What occurred was that, every night, when trying to fall asleep, when closing the eyes, the rape scene became clear in your memory, because of this it cried all nights. I said to the patient who seemed to be being good to come the therapy, since now it managed to sleep.

Isadora remained in therapy for a year and seven months and after this period the mother alleged do not there be anymore financial possibility to bring her, besides the assistance be free. The whole psychotherapy process elapsed with few interpretative sentences. They were small touches data with a lot of care, because I felt in the relation transference that any direct reference to the rape could be felt as an aggression, a new violence. Even the word rape only was told by me after Isadora itself, after fourteen therapy months, managed her to tell, giving myself thus the certainty of being him now ready to hear and also talk about the rape.

In June 1990, Lady Maria comes again talk with me to inform me that a husband niece, cousin, of Isadora, of fourteen years had tried to commit suicide because the grandfather abused sexually her since child. Said do not have told Isadora the suicide attempt reason, however it did an anonymous accusation to the delegate ship, which was reason for all the husband family, except the grandparents, interrupt relations with her and also with Isadora and the siblings. As the mother went telling about the rapes occurred inside the family, I could understand the "mother carelessness of Isadora in order her alone for the street in a district situated in the city periphery, violent considered.

In March 1991, after one year of therapy, Isadora told me to have decided to stop to going to church because a girl asked her: "It is true that was you... How is the name of that what happened to with me? I never manage to remind the name". Tell that it is difficult for her even pronounce the name than happened to you. She denies and tells that the name is ugly and eccentric, because of this we do not remind, also talk that I was ugly and eccentric that the young man made, just as the name that she could not tell. Then Isadora says: "It is Ra..." It looks me as who asks for help and I complete: "You..." And I return the same kind of looking that she had given me. For patient completes the syllable that fault, it repeats the word rape and gives a sigh. It comments soon after that this word is very same ugly and return to the subject that it talked previously.(...) After have managed to tell what before I was unpronounceable Isadora no longer wants to play or to play and, in the first session after having told the word rape, sits down in the couch for the first time. Now yet can talk.

In month in which it stayed without coming for the therapy, it told me she after, menstruated and it was frightened to the see the blood in her panties and, as that day was at home of a cousin, told her the occurred. The cousin sixteen year said that could be anemia. The next day decided to tell to the blood mother in her panties, and the mother said that I was not anything of more, than was menstruation. In other session exposes me that had discharge from a hospital of the gynecologist and I understand that it wants to also have as being cured of the therapy, but Isadora wants to continue, because there are "many things that comes in to my head that I want to tell you". Talks that the mother is who does not want it to bring her more. It reminds of the first time in which it saw me and told "If I did not have coming here I would be up to now in the arms of that (?)" doing reference to the psychologist who attended her in hospital. Tell that had to relate to the psychologist everything that happened, by several times, what left her compelled, but that she wanted same was to tell me, because I am different, "you do not keep asking anything". it wants to narrate me the rape, "to see I stop to feeling guilty", tells her.

It feels guilty to for having entered the young man's car". Points have been this "larger mistake", in spite of not caning guess what he would go to happen. Your mother, according to her, many times already had alerted you for never enter cars of strange. It relates me do not have been coerced to enter the car, that entered because he wanted, in spite of having told to all that out thank you. In this day had exited to buy a sandal. It was alone, because the mother was sewing and could not go together. When it investigated to the salesman on the sandal, he said do not there be anymore its number. So, when it went out from the store, a young man boarded her telling her have seen in an other store the sandal that she wished; The store stayed in an other district and he offered to lead her by car. She accepted and just regretted when the young man started to do you strange questions. It stayed with much fear and missed of air when he asked how she slept, if the father touched her "there" and another question that she tells already have forgotten, that when it realized that he was going by a way that carried to a highway started to cry and to ask so that he carried her however. But he threatened to kill case screamed, that if she did everything that he wanted, he then it would solve went to let her live or would kill her. It remembers accurately the location details where he carried her, and according to she in the middle of the woods there was a clean place, without grams and without trees, and says me believes that he carried other girls there, because it seemed to you that the location was already prepared for this end. It relates me that during the rape just keep thinking: "Why is he doing that with me?" It describes me still the pain that felt and that to decreased her started to think of God and then seemed that the fact was not happening most with herself, but with other person.

In the subsequent sessions to the rape description Isadora not only proceeded talking about the form more tranquility rape as to nominate the occurred with her as "abuse". Isadora also passed to sit down in the couch and to talk. He never more wanted to play or play. In some sessions opened its ludicrous box, it verified the content and turned to closes it (...) The patient's last session was in June 1991, however, I and Isadora ignored that it would be this our last encounter. I believe that the mother, when recognizing daughter's improvement boycotted the treatment, did not bring her more to the therapy. After several consecutive faults, without notice, she said finally me on the telephone that it could not bring most the daughter to the consultation room, due to the ticket increase by bus.

In the analysis of the clinical case the therapist adds that Isadora was generated in a family in which the three brothers of her father, still children, had been raped by the paternal grandfather, the even though submitted the cousin of Isadora the frequent sexual abuses, since its childhood until the adolescence. There is here a rape and incest overlapping, each one with your "concrete risks and your representations, fears and fantasies, conscious and unconscious those certainly circulate in the family and somehow determine your members' behaviors.

In the theoretical analysis of the case, the therapist seize upon Ferenzci's formulations, Freud and mostly of Herrmann. I present here just some, staying for those more interested the consultation to the original source. By Herrmann (1999) detaches the formulation that the adults who cohabit with the child have her own unconscious determinations, and they put them in action, know, in the son's treatment. We are born and we create us in a psychopathological kitchen, where they prepare the conflicts potentially neurosis's generators.

Of Ferenczi (1932/1966) takes advantage the idea that, in the largest part of the unconscious fantasies of many neurotic, the father appears as a predecessor in his sexual relations, concluding seem to there be in the families – especially in the of the mother – the belief in the rape inevitability. Of Freud (1913/1996) uses the barrier breaking idea of the incest, how much he affirms that the psychoanalysis discoveries turn the hypothesis of an innate aversion to the incestuous sexual totally unsustainable relation. They demonstrate, on the contrary, that human beings' most precocious sexual very new excitations are unavoidably of incestuous character. Such pulses would be halted by the repression, for which has been contributing along times the most several kinds of prohibitions – of religious order, heredity etc. In the family of Isadora, perhaps in function of the religious fanaticism, the religious prohibitions, the fear of the divine punishments or of the discrimination seems, for the therapist, have exercised an enormous weight. Something of the kind: "It is to be raped, that is by someone of outside". What belongs from within and is secret, is substituted whereby belongs to outside and public.

The therapist formulates that when knowing Isadora, already in the first interview, when she marks do not like talking about that I had occurred you, although knowing there to treat exactly than I had happened you, were already both involved by the psychoanalysis method. In spite of not having theories pre-established about by patient, setting itself, already defined and it turned possible the relation transfer and to let it arises to take in consideration, as it is understood the technique of the floating attention and of the neutrality in the Fields Theory. For the therapist, when during the process were appearing all the violence acts brandish against at patient: The first psychologist who attended her doing-to repeat several times the suffered rape as if it wanted to perpetuate it, so that the fact did not fall into the forgetfulness; the teacher, that showed the classroom colleagues the newspaper contend the rape reportage and identifying her for them as being her the victim; her mother, that told to all in the waiting room that she outside raped; Besides the imposed interdictions - do not watch television, school schedule's change etc -, like punishment form. Who is raped deserves to be punished; it seemed to suggest mother's posture. Such facts, as it warns the therapist, were important in your clinical conduct, and during great part of the sessions it abstained of doing direct references about the sexual violence suffered by the patient. While the therapeutic process went uncoiling itself, the therapist waited time of Isadora, limiting herself to pronounce interpretative sentences, with the care that they could not be felt by the patient like invasions, waiting with that her invigoration and the increase of your confidence.

Meltzer (1971), Ogden (1996), consider the psychoanalytical process as that in which analyzing it is created by means of a process inter-subjective similar to that present in the processes identification. An analysis is not considered by them simply a creation process of an analytic subject, that there was not before. The history of the analyzing is created in the transfer-contra transfer, in a continuous communication of inter-subjectivity, in which analytic process evolves and is interpreted by the analyst and by the patient. The psychoanalysis subject, from this done, takes it! Form and is created in the space inter-subjectivity between analyst and analyzing. With the end of the psychoanalytical therapy, the patient appropriates of inter-subjectivity of the analytic pair and transforms her in an internal dialog.

Chapter 7
Final Considerations

Final Considerations

They are countless the examples of clinical cases that could be here related, once are many the styles, the purposes and the contexts in which they are described. It would be impossible relate cases with its daily evolution, in other words, session by session. Each case summarizes a life and a life does not give to be told in all of its details, not only to for being unique, singular, in spite of controlling what there is of universal, common, profound and archetype in all human beings.

Write about Psychoanalysis seems to be an endless work. In the psychoanalysis does not exist an unique theory, some last decades and then they disappear. However, the psychoanalysis method remains and demonstrates its discoveries possibilities of the human soul. After all, the method is that propitiates the basic terms of discovery of new theories. The theories guide the technique, that by its side, it is going to find countless unused clinical situations that, when generalized and abstracted of immediate experience, it transforms in theory.

I think, and I search in my own experience, that the difficult to admit is that the Psychoanalysis invents every minute. The new that is presented did not give by itself, by spontaneous generation, by a profound and brilliant comprehension of a thinker isolated of everything and above all, but that was determined. In other words, that I was possible being, among others possible, it materialized in a theoretical formulation, in a technical innovation. Such possibility was created by the discoveries potentialities of its own method.

If the answer is in the method, the Psychoanalysis paid by its preservation a high price, losing cultured, valorous, creative men. Freud along his life did not abandon the psychoanalysis method. Nowadays evaluate that the method clearing attempts, by more difficult, confused or simplistic that can seem, they are concrete acts of love, of respect and that has for main goal the Psychoanalysis preservation. This can, at this moment so disturbed of the history, leave its first childhood with technical and theoretical elements endowed of capacities to support mutability that life in the reserve.

Appendex - I
Bibliograhic References

Aberastury, A. (1983). Adolescência. Em Aberastury, A. & cols. (Orgs.). *Adolescência*.(pp. 15-32). Porto Alegre: Artes Médicas.

Aberastury, A. (1984). A percepção da morte na criança. Em Aberastury, A. & cols. (Orgs.) *A Percepção da Morte na Criança e Outros Escritos*. (pp.128-139). Porto Alegre: Artes Médicas.

Abraham, K. (1970). *Teoria Psicanalítica da Libido: Sobre o Caráter e o Desenvolvimento da Libido*. Rio de Janeiro: Imago.

Allport, G. W. (1976). *Personalidade*. São Paulo: Edusp.

American Psychiatric Association. (APA). (1995). *Manual Diagnóstico e Estatístico de Transtornos Mentais*. Porto Alegre: Artes Médicas

Beck, A. T. (1967). *Depression: Clinical, experimental and theoretical aspects*. New York: Herper & Row.

Bleger, J. (1969). *Psicologia da Conduta*. Porto Alegre: Artes Médicas.

Blos, P. (1985). *Adolescência: Uma Interpretação Psicanalítica*. Rio de Janeiro: Martins Fontes.

Brenner, C. (1969). *Noções Básicas de Psicanálise*. Rio de Janeiro: Imago.

Carvalho, U.S. de.(2004). *A Supervisão Psicanalítica*. São Paulo: Casa do Psicólogo.

Charan, I. O . (1990). *Estupro e o Assédio Sexual*. Rio de Janeiro: Ed. Rosa dos Tempos.

Chabrol, H. (1990). *A Depressão do Adolescente*. Campinas: Papirus

Dorsch, F., Häcker, H. & Stapf, K-H.(2001). *Dicionário de Psicologia Dorsch*. Petrópolis: Vozes.

Ebert, M. H., Loosen, P. T. & Nurcombe, B. (2002). *Psiquiatria: Diagnóstico e Tratamento*. Porto Alegre: Artmed Editora.

Erikson, E. H. (1998). Erikson, E.H. (1998) *O Ciclo de Vida Completo*. Porto Alegre: Artes Médicas.

Etchegoyen, R. H. (1989). *Fundamentos da Técnica Psicanalítica*. Porto Alegre: Artes Médicas.

Fenichel, O. (1981). *Teoria Psicanalítica das Neuroses*. São Paulo: Atheneu.

Feijó, R. B.; & Chaves, M. L. F. (2002). Comportamento suicida. Em Costa, M. C. O. & Souza, R. P. de.(Orgs.). *Adolescência: Aspectos Clínicos e Psicossociais*. (pp. 398-408). Porto Alegre: Artmed.

Ferenczi, S. (1919/1992). Psicanálise. Em: *Obras Completa*, vol. IV. São Paulo: Martins Fontes.

Ferenczi, S. (1932/1966). *Problemas y metodos del psicoanalisis*. Buenos Aires: Paidós.

Fichte, J. S. (1980). *Os Pensadores*. São Paulo: Abril Cultural.

Freud, F.(1896/1996). Novas Observações Sobre as Neuropsicoses de Defesa. *Em Obras Completas*, Vol 3. Rio de Janeiro: Imago.

Freud, S. (1914/1996a). Sobre o Narcisismo: uma introdução. *Obras Completas*, vol. 14. Rio de Janeiro: Imago.

Freud, S. (1910/1996). Cinco lições de psicanálise. *Obras Completas,* vol. 11. Rio de Janeiro: Imago.

Freud, S. (1910/1996b). Contribuições a uma discussão sobre o suicídio. *Obras Completas*, Vol. 11. Rio de Janeiro: Imago.

Freud, S. (1912/1996). Recomendações aos médicos que exercem a psicanálise. Em *Obras Completas*, vol. 12. Rio de Janeiro: Imago.

Freud, S. (1913/1996). Sobre o Início do Tratamento. Em *Obras Completas*, vol. 12. Rio de Janeiro: Imago.

Freud, S. (1915/1996c). Luto e Melancolia. *Obras Completas*, Vol. 14. Rio de janeiro: Imago.

Freud, S. (1920/1996). Além do Princípio do Prazer. *Obras Completas*, Vol. 18. Rio de Janeiro: Imago.

Freud, S. (1923/1996). O Ego e o ID. *Obras Completas*, Vol. 19. Rio de Janeiro: Imago.

Freud, S. (1926/1996). Inibições, Sintomas e Angústia. *Obras Completas*, Vol. 20. Rio de Janeiro: Imago.

Freud, S. (1933/1996). Psicanálise e ocultismo. *Obras Completas,*Vol. 22. Rio de Janeiro: Imago.
Freud, S. (1939/1996). Análise Terminável e Interminável. *Obras Completas*, Vol. 23. Rio de Janeiro: Imago.

Furniss, T. (1993). *Abuso Sexual da Criança: uma abordagem multidisciplinar.* Porto Alegre: Artes Médicas.

Gabbard, G. O. (1998). *Psiquiatria Psicodinâmica. Baseado no DSM-IV*. Porto Alegre: Artes Médicas.

Goethe, J. W. (1983). *Fausto*. São Paulo: Editora Abril.

Goethe, J. W. (1983). *Werther*. São Paulo: Editora Abril.

Herrmann, F. (1991). O Método da Psicanálise: Andaimes do Real. São Paulo: Brasiliense.

Herrmann, F. (1991). Clínica Psicanalítica: A Arte da Interpretação. São Paulo: Brasiliense.

Herrmann, F. (1999). *A Psique e o Eu.* São Paulo: Hepyché.

Herrmann, F. (2001). *Introdução à Teoria dos Campos*. São Paulo: Casa do Psicólogo.

Jung, C. G. (1982a). Aion: Estudos sobre o simbolismo do si-mesmo. *Obras Completas*, vol. 9/2. Petrópolis: Vozes.

Jung, C. G. (1982b). Tipos Psicológicos. *Obras Completas*, Vol. 6. Petrópolis: Vozes.

Kalina, E. (1983). O processo diagnóstico em psicanálise de adolescentes. Em Aberastury e cols.(Orgs.). *Adolescência.*(pp. 93-109). Porto Alegre: Artes Médicas.

Kalina, E. (1999). *Psicoterapia de Adolescentes: Teoria, técnica e casos clínicos*. Porto Alegre: Artmed.

Khan, M. M. R.(1977). *Psicanálise: teoria, técnica e casos clínicos*. Rio de Janeiro: Francisco Alves.

Kaplan, H., Sadock, B. J. & Grebb, J. A. (1997). *Compêndio de Psiquiatria: Ciência do Comportamento e Psiquiatria Clínica*. Porto Alegre: Artes Médica.

Klein, M. (1982). Notas sobre Alguns Mecanismos Esquizóides. Em Riviere, J. (Org.). *Os Progressos da Psicanálise*.(pp.313-343). Rio de Janeiro: Zahar.

Knobel, M. (1983). A adolescência e o tratamento psicanalítico de adolescentes. Em Em Aberastury, A. & cols. (Orgs.). *Adolescência.*(pp. 111-142). Porto Alegre: Artes Médicas.

Krech, D. & Crutchield, R. (1974). *Elementos de Psicologia.* 5ª ed. São Paulo: Pioneira.

Laplanche, J. (1988). *Teoria da Sedução Generalizada.* Porto Alegre: Artes Médicas.

Laplanche, J.& Pontalis, J- B. *Vocabulário da Psicanálise.* São Paulo: Martins Fontes.

Levisky, D. L. (1998). *Adolescência: Reflexões Psicanalíticas.* São Paulo: Casa do Psicólogo.

Lindner, R. (1972). *A Hora de Cinqüenta Minutos.* Rio de Janeiro: Imago.

Macknnon, R. A.& Michels, R. (1992). *A Entrevista Psiquiátrica na prática diária.* Porto Alegre: Artes Médicas.

Marcelli, D. (1998). *Manual de Psicopatologia da Infância de Ajuriaguerra.* Porto Alegre: Artes Médicas.

Meltzer, D. (1971). *O Processo Psicanalítico. Da Criança ao Adulto.* Rio de Janeiro: Imago.

Mendels, J.(1972). *Conceitos de Depressão.* Rio de Janeiro: LTC Editora.

Menninguer, K. A. & Holzman, P. S. (1979). *Teoria da Técnica Psicanalítica.* Rio de Janeiro: Zahar.

Mezan, R. (2001). *Freud: a trama dos conceitos.* São Paulo: Perspectiva.

Mezan, R. (1993). *A Sombra de Don Juan.* São Paulo: Brasiliense.

Mezan, R. (1988). *A Vingança da Esfinge: Ensaios de Psicanálise.* São Paulo: Brasiliense.

Nunberg, H. (1989). *Princípios da Psicanálise.* São Paulo: Atheneu.

Ogden, T. (1996). *Os Sujeitos da Psicanálise.* São Paulo: Casa do Psicólogo.

Organização Mundial de Saúde (OMS). (1993*). Classificação de transtornos mentais e do comportamento da CID – 10.* Porto Alegre: Artes Médicas

Paz, L. R. de. (1983). Adolescência. Crise e dessimbiotização. Em Aberastury e cols.(Orgs.). Adolescência.(pp. 165-184). Porto Alegre: Artes Médicas.

Reich, W. A. (1975). *Função do Orgasmo.* São Paulo: Brasiliense.

Shakespeare, W. (1987). *Obras Completas.* Madri: Aguilar.

Segal, H. (1975). *Introdução à Obra de Melanie Klein.* Rio de Janeiro: Imago.

Silva, R. A. S. da. (2004). *A Teoria dos Campos e a Violência Sexual: Um estudo Psicanalítico.* Dissertação de Mestrado, Faculdade de Psicologia, Pontifícia Universidade Católica de São Paulo, São Paulo.

Solomon, A. (2002) O Demônio do Meio-Dia: Uma Anatomia da Depressão. Rio de Janeiro: Objetiva.

Spitz, R. (1993). *O Primeiro ano de vida.* São Paulo: Martins Fontes.

Turato, C. R. (2003). *Tratado da metodologia da pesquisa clínico-qualitativa.* Petrópolis,: Vozes.

Tuckett, D. (1993). Some thoughts on the presentation and discussion of the clinical material of psychoanalysis. *Int. J. Psycho-Anal., 74, 1175-1189.*

Winnicott, D. W. (1975). *O Brincar & a Realidade.* Rio de Janeiro: Imago.

Appendex - II
About Author

Claudio Garcia Capitão is psychologist and psychoanalyst, with specialization in clinical psychology and in hospitable psychology. Nowadays he teaches in the graduation courses and post graduation stricto Sensu in University San Francisco, Sao Paulo, Brazil. He works as psychologist in the Institute of Infectious Disease Emilio Ribas attending patient bearers of HIV/Aids, has countless chapters' books and articles published in the main Brazilian scientific magazines.

Appendex - III
Index

A

Aberastury · - 67 -, - 115 -, - 116 -, - 117 -
Abraham · - 60 -, - 62 -, - 64 -, - 65 -, - 115 -
America · 4
American · - 115 -
Anguish · - 5 -, - 8 -, - 9 -, - 10 -, - 12 -, - 13 -, - 14 -, - 16 -, - 23 -, - 26 -, - 38 -, - 65 -, - 66 -, - 68 -, - 71 -, - 76 -, - 79 -, - 84 -, - 88 -, - 93 -, - 96 -, - 99 -, - 103 -, - 104 -
Approach · - 1 -
Author · - 2 -, - 119 -

B

Beck · - 59 -, - 115 -
Bleger, j · - 115 -

C

Carvalho, u.s · - 115 -
Cases · - 2 -, - 81 -, - 91 -
Childhood · - 1 -, - 65 -
Cid · - 2 -, - 101 -, - 117 -
Claudio · - 119 -
Clinic · - 2 -, - 78 -, - 81 -
Clinical · - 2 -, - 24 -, - 91 -, - 99 -, - 101 -, - 102 -, - 105 -, - 107 -, - 115 -
Conscious · - 1 -, - 2 -, - 4 -, - 6 -, - 7 -, - 8 -, - 9 -, - 16 -, - 22 -, - 29 -, - 30 -, - 31 -, - 32 -, - 34 -, - 36 -, - 37 -, - 49 -, - 58 -, - 60 -, - 61 -, - 66 -, - 73 -, - 81 -, - 82 -, - 84 -, - 88 -, - 95 -, - 99 -, - 111 -
Consideration · - 1 -
Constitution · - 1 -, - 46 -, - 47 -, - 50 -, - 51 -, - 65 -, - 67 -, - 69 -, - 77 -

---

D

Damage · - 3 -
Degree · - 3 -, - 4 -, - 5 -, - 11 -, - 15 -, - 69 -, - 85 -
Depression · - 1 -, - 57 -, - 65 -, - 67 -, - 115 -
Displeasure · - 2 -, - 3 -, - 4 -, - 9 -, - 12 -, - 16 -, - 84 -

---

E

Express · - 1 -, - 20 -, - 23 -, - 24 -, - 54 -, - 59 -, - 70 -, - 71 -, - 89 -, - 93 -, - 103 -

---

F

First · 4, - 1 -, - 3 -, - 29 -
Fish · - 19 -, - 20 -, - 21 -
Forms · - 1 -, - 8 -, - 10 -, - 19 -, - 26 -, - 28 -, - 32 -, - 39 -, - 43 -, - 45 -, - 64 -, - 66 -, - 76 -, - 77 -, - 79 -, - 80 -, - 82 -, - 90 -, - 100 -

Freud · 7, - 1 -, - 2 -, - 3 -, - 4 -, - 5 -, - 6 -, - 7 -, - 8 -, - 9 -, - 10 -, - 11 -, - 12 -, - 13 -, - 14 -, - 15 -, - 16 -, - 17 -, - 20 -, - 22 -, - 30 -, - 31 -, - 32 -, - 33 -, - 34 -, - 37 -, - 38 -, - 39 -, - 41 -, - 42 -, - 43 -, - 47 -, - 48 -, - 49 -, - 50 -, - 51 -, - 60 -, - 61 -, - 62 -, - 63 -, - 64 -, - 65 -, - 68 -, - 69 -, - 77 -, - 82 -, - 83 -, - 85 -, - 86 -, - 88 -, - 89 -, - 90 -, - 95 -, - 107 -, - 111 -, - 113 -, - 116 -, - 117 -

---

H

Herrmann, F · - 116 -
History · - 1 -, - 7 -, - 11 -, - 25 -, - 33 -, - 36 -, - 53 -, - 55 -, - 67 -, - 75 -, - 76 -, - 77 -, - 78 -, - 79 -, - 81 -, - 82 -, - 83 -, - 84 -, - 88 -, - 89 -, - 91 -, - 92 -, - 96 -, - 98 -, - 101 -, - 102 -, - 103 -, - 105 -, - 112 -, - 113 -
Human · 7, - 1 -, - 3 -, - 4 -, - 5 -, - 8 -, - 13 -, - 21 -, - 28 -, - 32 -, - 34 -, - 36 -, - 39 -, - 40 -, - 44 -, - 45 -, - 46 -, - 47 -, - 50 -, - 51 -, - 52 -, - 54 -, - 59 -, - 63 -, - 67 -, - 73 -, - 74 -, - 75 -, - 77 -, - 78 -, - 80 -, - 81 -, - 96 -, - 98 -, - 100 -, - 101 -, - 107 -, - 111 -, - 113 -

---

I

Images · - 1 -, - 24 -, - 51 -, - 81 -
Interpretation · - 1 -, - 2 -, - 37 -, - 50 -, - 77 -, - 78 -, - 99 -
Introduction · - 1 -

M

Maria's · - 2 -
Method · - 1 -, - 29 -, - 37 -

N

Nurcombe · - 59 -, - 84 -, - 115 -

O

Oedipus · - 1 -, - 7 -, - 8 -, - 10 -, - 11 -, - 28 -, - 30 -, - 33 -, - 44 -, - 51 -, - 61 -, - 68 -, - 94 -, - 95 -, - 104 -, - 107 -
Organic · - 2 -, - 105 -

P

Psychic · 7, - 1 -, - 2 -, - 4 -, - 6 -, - 7 -, - 9 -, - 17 -, - 22 -, - 23 -, - 26 -, - 28 -, - 29 -, - 30 -, - 31 -, - 39 -, - 40 -, - 43 -, - 47 -, - 50 -, - 51 -, - 52 -, - 53 -, - 54 -, - 55 -, - 58 -, - 59 -, - 60 -, - 61 -, - 64 -, - 66 -, - 67 -, - 68 -, - 72 -, - 73 -, - 74 -, - 75 -, - 76 -, - 77 -, - 80 -, - 81 -, - 82 -, - 83 -, - 84 -, - 85 -, - 87 -, - 88 -, - 89 -, - 90 -, - 93 -, - 94 -, - 98 -, - 101 -, - 102 -, - 104 -, - 107 -
Psychoanalysis · 7, - 1 -, - 24 -, - 29 -, - 31 -, - 34 -, - 36 -, - 37 -, - 39 -, - 43 -, - 44 -, - 48 -, - 75 -, - 77 -, - 78 -, - 95 -, - 113 -
Psychoanalytical · - 1 -, - 19 -, - 21 -, - 24 -, - 77 -, - 78 -, - 99 -, - 105 -

R

Rape · - 2 -, - 107 -
References · - 2 -, - 115 -
Representation · - 2 -, - 78 -
Resistance · - 2 -, - 3 -, - 4 -, - 5 -, - 6 -, - 14 -, - 16 -, - 17 -, - 20 -, - 35 -, - 84 -, - 85 -, - 86 -, - 95 -, - 106 -
Rupture · 7, - 1 -, - 2 -, - 23 -, - 27 -, - 78 -

S

Satisfaction · - 2 -, - 3 -, - 5 -, - 9 -, - 10 -, - 11 -, - 22 -, - 30 -, - 32 -, - 60 -, - 61 -, - 87 -, - 93 -, - 98 -
Schools · - 1 -, - 28 -, - 34 -, - 45 -, - 68 -
Scratch · - 2 -, - 99 -
Services · 4
Symbolize · - 1 -
Symptoms · - 2 -, - 3 -, - 10 -, - 11 -, - 12 -, - 13 -, - 14 -, - 26 -, - 49 -, - 54 -, - 57 -, - 64 -, - 67 -, - 69 -, - 70 -, - 81 -, - 83 -, - 87 -, - 88 -, - 89 -, - 90 -, - 91 -, - 93 -, - 97 -, - 98 -, - 101 -, - 102 -, - 104 -, - 105 -, - 106 -

T

Theoretical · - 1 -, - 44 -

V

Violence · - 1 -, - 44 -, - 46 -